THE RIVER REMEMBERS

To Ben Hauff - this
chronicle about our
mutual heritage -

With love -
S. L. Shneiderman
May 2, 1984

BY THE SAME AUTHOR

Between Fear and Hope
The Warsaw Heresy

S. L. SHNEIDERMAN

THE RIVER REMEMBERS

HORIZON PRESS *New York*

The author wishes to acknowledge gratitude to Joseph Singer and Shulamit R. Charney for their translation of portions of this book and to Charles J. Azenberg for his encouragement.

The Yiddish edition of *The River Remembers* received the International Bergen-Belsen Remembrance Award.

To my wife and collaborator Eileen,
to our children Helen and Ben,
and to their children—
this chronicle of our heritage

CONTENTS

ILLUSTRATIONS

1

AFTER THE FLOOD

The Vistula is to Poland what the Mississippi is to America and the Volga is to Russia. In this story the Vistula emerges as the river on whose banks Jews lived for centuries, developed their own civilization and perished in the most ghastly way recorded in history.

Throughout the years of the Second World War I constantly returned to Kazimierz in my thoughts. I knew that no Jews were left in my home town on the right bank of the Vistula. Yet I always had a vision of them in their black gabardines and round hats, milling about the marketplace. In the background were the stone houses, colored blue, white, purple and green.

The human-like faces of lions, deer, birds and fish, painted on the high, vaulted ceiling of the old synagogue, also lived on in my mind. Even the Christian saints in bas-relief on the facades of the Renaissance mansions aroused nostalgia in me. The gigantic figure of Saint Christopher, striding through a flood with a tree in his hand, animated my dreams and became a symbol of the Nazi deluge. The saint carries one child on his shoulder, and the heads of three others peep out of a pouch attached to his waist. The water only reaches his ankles and crabs bite at his heels.

When I made my first trip to Poland shortly after the Liberation, I kept putting off a visit to my birthplace. The desolation of the Warsaw Ghetto, the piles of ashes and rubble in the obliterated Jewish streets, stifled the urge to see my home town. I was afraid to confront the reality. I had learned the truth when I had unexpectedly come across some of my compatriots in Lower Silesia, where the few surviving Jews from nearly all of Poland had gathered.

Early one morning a knock at my door in the Metropol Hotel in Wroclaw suddenly awakened me; in an instant the fantastic web of my strange dream vanished. I had seen many rooms in Kazimierz houses. People wandered around in them. In the center was the drawing room of the town's rich man, Vovtche Bromberg, its huge, old wall clock showing the movement of the stars. It began to disintegrate abruptly, the hands dashed all around wildly, and the dial was transformed into the face of a grotesque prankster whose giggling fused with the knocking as it became more insistent.

When I opened the door, a former home town acquaintance stood there — Moshe Reisman. We had not seen each other for some thirty years, but I recognized him immediately because he looked so much like his father, the town scribe. It seemed to me that the pale, anxiety-ridden face before me, with its peering eyes and thick brows, had shaken off the long, red beard and curly earlocks that his father wore. His bowed spine and odd manner also recalled his father's. Although Reisman had been a heretic in his youth, he had helped his father inscribe the Torah scrolls.

He proceeded to unfold the tragic tale of our *shtetl*,* and told me how my brothers and their families had died. He mentioned the names of Poles in whose care the holy objects from the synagogue had been left. Then he made a quick transition to present-day Poland, and threw back at me with disgust my critical observations that all human values were being trampled under the communist regime.

Shtetl: a small-town Jewish community in Eastern Europe. The plural is *shtetlekh*.

Before my meeting with Moshe Reisman, I had heard that he had been maltreated in the Soviet Union despite the long sentence he had served in a Polish prison for his pre-war communist activities. I was astounded that he had not grown disillusioned with communism, although it had dealt him such a harsh blow. He laughed appreciatively when I suggested a parallel: just as his father became more pious the greater his poverty, so he, the son, embraced communism more fervently the more blatant its failures. Reisman conceded that even Soviet communism, let alone the Polish brand which he termed the "first phase of the socialist order," was far from perfect. But he blamed this on the "careerists," who managed to live comfortably in the interim.

"I'm a simple soldier," he announced with pride, "and want to put my own conscience in order first."

When I asked him how his conscience squared with the crimes of the communist regimes, he waved his hand impatiently:

"Let's not talk about that. We won't agree anyway."

He cut the topic short by inquiring about Kazimierz acquaintances in America. He wanted to hear all the details, how they lived, how their children were being raised.

Reisman refused my offers of help though it was obvious from his appearance that he could hardly clothe himself out of his meager earnings as a bookbinder. He had sacrificed the best years of his youth for the communist cause, and still dreamed of "social justice." He was not even distressed by the fact that the anti-Semitism still prevailing in the People's Republic of Poland prevented him from going back to his birthplace, so that he had to make a new life for himself in German Lower Silesia. He did not urge me to visit Kazimierz either, although he felt that my American war correspondent's uniform would keep me from harm. His reference to my uniform was tinged with a sarcastic overtone.

After much hesitation I finally decided to go to Kazimierz. Then the 1946 Kielce pogrom erupted. Forty-two Jewish men, women, and children were slaughtered in broad daylight by a mob that had been whipped up by the medieval canard of ritual murder. The fires in the Nazi crematoria on Polish soil had barely been extinguished; the pain of Auschwitz, Maidanek, Belzec and Treblinka was still acute.

From Kielce the raging pogroms swept to other towns and cities. On one of those turbulent days, I met my early childhood teacher, Sonia Szenderowicz-Wisnia, on a Warsaw street. We used to call her Sonia, an intimacy between mentor and pupils that was part of the pedagogic experiment she instituted in her school, and helped to bind several generations of Jewish youth to her with long-term admiration and affection. She had just returned from Kazimierz, her first visit there since the Liberation. Her Polish friends had begged her to leave before nightfall, since the area swarmed with underground nationalist bands which never ceased to ferret out surviving Jews, although the communist regime had already been in power for two years.

Sonia and her two daughters belonged to the handful of Kazimierz Jews who had escaped to Janowiec on the other side of the Vistula on Passover eve in 1942, when the Kazimierz ghetto was finally liquidated. Her husband, Shimon, the Hebrew language teacher in town, believed like many others that the Germans would only hunt down Jewish men. So he had left his family behind in Kazimierz, crossed the Bug River into Soviet-occupied Poland, and for a while lived in Kowel. Following the invasion of Soviet Russia, he shared the fate of thousands of Polish Jews, who perished during their flight from the Nazis.

My teacher told me of her wanderings through the towns of Poland until she reached Warsaw, where Christian friends found her a job, first as cook and later as private teacher in a village outside Kielce. She stayed there until the Liberation. Her oldest daughter, Mita, also found refuge in Warsaw with a Polish friend, while the younger Rina was hidden in a convent. After the war was over, Rina at first refused to be parted from her Christian friends, like hundreds of other Jewish youngsters.

Weary and broken by her shattering experiences during the five years of Nazi occupation, Sonia lacked the strength to look for a new home outside of Poland, but the Kielce pogrom forced her to a decision. She and her younger daughter sneaked across the border to Austria, and traveled from there to Palestine on an illegal ship. That last evening before her flight from the country, Sonia said to me with unrestrained bitterness:

"For me, the Kazimierz chapter ended after my pupils, Zalman

The facade of the Przybylo mansion in the marketplace, where the town's archives are kept. The gigantic figure of Saint Christopher strides through the water.

Ashkenazi and Samuel Goldfarb, came out of hiding and were murdered on the thresholds of their homes. If this could happen in our town, there is no hope left for us Jews in Poland."

In Kielce I saw the mutilated corpses of the victims, and came face to face with the killers in the courtroom. Their eyes were fixed on their murder weapons—the crowbars and axes that lay on the judge's table as proof of their infamy. Yet I could not picture an axe descending upon the head of a Jew in my home town, where Jews had for centuries lived peacefully next door to their Christian neighbors.

As we said goodby to each other, Sonia warned me not to visit Kazimierz. But if I did ever go there, she added in the same breath, would I photograph the monument on the grave of her parents and younger brother, Zygmunt Szenderowicz.

"That's one of the few tombstones left from the new cemetery," she said. "It was simply razed, and the synagogue is nothing but four bare walls."

Two days after my meeting with Sonia, a young, medium-built woman with dyed blonde hair and hardened features came to see me at the Polonia, the only hotel left in gutted Warsaw. Her Polish name was unfamiliar to me, but the moment she mentioned her real name, the lines in her face changed and I recognized my former schoolmate, Reizl Levine. I had not seen her for some fifteen years. But I had heard rumors of her communist activities, and of the strike she had organized in the brewery in Rogow, a village outside Kazimierz known as the region's "red nest." Shortly before the war, she had been arrested and sentenced to several years in prison. The last news of her had come to me at an unexpected meeting with her elder brother, Moshe Levine, a volunteer in the Polish Dąbrowski Battalion of the International Brigade during the Spanish Civil War. It was December 1937 in besieged Madrid. The mountains around the Manzanares River were covered with snow—a winter scene resembling our home town on the Vistula.

When I told Reizl about her brother who was killed a few days after our meeting in Republican Spain, she dabbed her eyes with a handkerchief. Then, biting her lips, she whispered: "No more tears left . . ." After a while she almost shouted: "I want to get out of

here. Help me! But I don't want to smuggle across the border. I
don't want to leave Poland illegally."

Like Sonia, she warned me not to go to Kazimierz under any
circumstances. Then, bitterly and without ceremony, she told me
her experiences during the occupation. In Rogow, some five miles
from Kazimierz where she had organized communist cells for
years, she had managed to find a hiding place—for herself only,
none for her family. Shortly afterwards she was forced to leave the
village; the peasant who was sheltering her was warned to get rid of
"his Jewess." While she was there she had daily observed peasants
passing by with wagons full of loot from neighboring Jewish
shtetlekh.

"I came back to Kazimierz," she went on, "and found two
ghettoes there: one in the street where the community bathhouse
was, the other on Nadrzeczna Street. My father was no longer
alive. He was one of dozens killed the day the Jewish population
was herded into the ghetto. I found my mother and three younger
brothers in a single room, which they shared with two other
families. There was no space for me, and I went to a Polish friend in
Warsaw who had been arrested with me during the strike."

As if in a trance, she described the hardships she underwent
looking for a haven, her participation in the general Warsaw uprising in August 1944, and more hiding in ruins and cellars until the
Liberation.

"I never went back to Kazimierz," she said. In a peremptory
voice she repeated:

"Don't dare go there. The whole region swarms with underground gangs."

2

"YOU SHALL NOT CROSS OVER
INTO IT"

Despite the warnings, I started off for Kazimierz. It was my first train journey in postwar Poland. The familiar names of towns along the way stirred recollections of the times when Jews were bustling about with packages, getting on and off at stations such as Otwock and Dęblin. But this August 1946 the platforms were deserted. The run-down, discolored coaches were half empty, and I vainly sought a Jewish face among the travelers.

In Gołąb, a patrol of three armed men came aboard to inspect the passengers' papers. After they had gone, the conductor, who had been holding a lengthy discussion with me, breathed a sigh of relief. He whispered that such "inspections" had been carried out more than once between Warsaw and Lublin by the "men of the forest." He was referring to the anti-government, underground bands who wore the same uniforms as the new Polish army. He added that, during some of these "inspections," travelers, whose documents showed that they were communist officials or Jews, had been spirited away.

At last, the train chugged into Pulawy, the final stop before Kazimierz. I saw the familiar brick and wood station building densely overgrown with ivy beginning to turn an autumnal red. There were the usual boxes of multicolored nasturtiums on the window-sills of the upper floors, and on the edge of the roof I saw the same pigeon coop, with cooing doves perched around it. It seemed to me that even the stooped, elderly stationmaster was the same, and that his red cap had merely faded.

Only two women got off the train with me; no one got on. My heart pounding, I looked at the peeling walls of the station that had been the gateway to the outside world in my youthful dreams. There was not a living soul in the restaurant apart from the aged woman behind the counter. She wore a stained, white jacket and shooed flies off the dishes. When I asked her how long she had been working there, she thought a moment:

"About thirty years." She also confirmed my guess that the stationmaster was the same old man.

"And are the portraits on the walls pre-war too?" I asked, pretending not to know.

The woman's grayish, furrowed face broke into a smile, and she explained: "Oh, no . . ." Army Chief Marshal Rydz-Smigly's picture had been replaced by Marshal Rola-Zymierski's, and President Moscicki's by President Boleslaw Bierut's.

The courtyard on the other side of the station was deserted, too. At one time carriages and droshkies had waited there, and Jewish coachmen had carried the bundles of arriving passengers. Now a single taxi was parked there: a dilapidated Soviet *Pobeda*. The driver, a husky young Pole, was not anxious to take me to Kazimierz for a few hours and then drive me back for the evening train to Warsaw. After I had agreed to his price, he said he could not guarantee getting into Kazimierz, since the town had been rent by disturbances in the past few days.

I sat down next to him. The cab sped along the pitted highway which was as familiar to me as the inns and churches coming into view at the entrance to every village. Not a trace remained of the Nazi madness that had raged over this land. Above the low shacks with their thatched, moss-covered roofs, I saw newly-built stone houses on the hillsides—proof of the growing prosperity of the peasants. Beyond the village of Wlostowice, over to the right, I could see the broad, lazy Vistula and its sandy islets; and on our left, a chain of gently sloping hills with orchards abounding in ripe fruit, red apples, golden pears and blue plums. And now the highway narrowed into a road bordered by huge, stout poplars with wartlike growths, evidence of their great age. Their thick branches and dense foliage shaded the road on that hot late summer day, providing delightful relief.

As we approached the Bochotnica bridge, we saw tents pitched on both sides of the river, and camouflaged machine gun nests nearby. We were stopped by a military patrol. An officer examined our papers and forbade us to go any farther. I asked for the reason, but he would not at first answer. When I explained the purpose of my journey, he grew more talkative, and told me that Kazimierz was in a state of siege. The night before there had been a confrontation with an armed band that had taken over the monastery and set up barricades there. The officer's words sounded strange in the idyllic atmosphere of Bochotnica village.

Just a few dozen paces from the bridge one could hear the rushing waterfall by the mill. It had belonged to Ezekiel Fried, whose large family had once shared the comfortable house nearby, and to which additional wings had been built after every wedding und each birth. As far as I could tell, none of these imposing dwellings had been harmed. The huge wooden mill-wheel was at a standstill. I had the feeling that time had stopped. The white ruins of the mountain castle that King Kazimierz (Casimir) the Great, the 14th century benevolent ruler of Poland, had built for his Jewish mistress, Esther, stood as before. The walls with their arched windows and massive escarpments were overgrown with entangled shrubs and weeds, and gave one the impression of a crown resting upon wildly dishevelled hair.

The royal ruins, the mill and, barely three miles beyond, my home town, were on the other side of the Bochotnica "Jordan." But the bridge barred my access to them. I recalled the Biblical admonition: "You shall not cross over into it." (Deut. 34:4)

3

KAZIMIERZ WITHOUT JEWS

A full ten years later, in December 1955, I finally got to Kazimierz, just before the turbulent Poznan strikes which led to the bloodless overthrow of the police regime in October 1956. The mood of rebellion had already permeated the works of leading Polish poets, particularly Adam Wazyk, whose "Poem for Adults" unmasked the duplicity and crimes of Stalinism. Wazyk told me that he had written this poem in Kazimierz during the summer of 1955.

This time I made the whole journey from Warsaw to my birthplace by car. I traveled through the obliterated Jewish communities of Otwock, Garwolin, Ryki, Korow, and Pulawy. The marketplace in Kazimierz was deserted. It was a sunny, chilly day, and the dry snow crunched beneath my feet. There were few people about; the icy surface reflected their shadows. The very first sight of the rebuilt, multicolored facades of the historic mansions I remembered shattered my dreams. I had the feeling that I was looking at a plaster model of the former town, although the vaulted roofs of the stone buildings and the balconies of the wooden houses were real enough. The unreality was due to the total absence of Jews, whose faces seemed to emerge from windows and doors everywhere. The Danzig House where I was born and raised had been restored too, but the apartments inside were evidently not ready for occupation. I was thus spared having to face the people who would take over the home from which my parents had been driven into the ghetto.

The old synagogue and its architectural ornamentation had also been restored, but at the entrance to its hall, where the weekly handwritten calendar of religious services used to hang, there was now a printed notice announcing a showing of the English film, *Mary Stuart*.

The first to recognize me was the former town elder, Jan Pisula, now dressed in a patched sheepskin and a mangy fur hat that matched the gray bristles on his unshaven face. He greeted me in Yiddish, and promptly asked if anyone in my family had been saved. He told me that he had seen my father on the day the *shtetl's* Jews were driven into the ghetto.

Pisula had had the annual privilege of buying the *chometz*, the leavened foods forbidden in Jewish homes after the onset of Passover. He spoke idiomatic Yiddish including Hebrew expressions without the slightest mispronunciation. He was familiar with the legends current among the Jews in the shtetl. When curious people stopped to ask about the stranger who had come to town in an automobile, Pisula took my arm and walked me up the hill toward the ruins of the royal palace.

"These are all Johnny-come-latelys, party activists; you've got to watch your step with them," the aged Pisula said, wiping away the tears caused by the biting frost. He told me some amusing stories about the new town leaders and the cooperatives where the food rotted and the goods were pilfered. Then he commented: "There's no longer any real life in Kazimierz without the Jews"—a remark which finally gave me the courage to ask why no Jews had managed to hide from the Nazis in Kazimierz.

"It couldn't be done, it couldn't be done," Pisula said haltingly. "As soon as the ghetto was set up, peasants from the neighboring villages seemed to sprout out of the ground. They grabbed the Jewish homes. We were terrified of them."

Back from our stroll to the royal ruins, I walked the streets and squares of the town where I vainly sought some traces of its former Jewish existence. Outside the historic synagogue I found no other mementoes of the *shtetl* either. The ancient stone house of worship; Reb Ezekiel's Hasidic Court with its carved, wooden columns by the front door; Reb Mottele's mansion; the almshouse for the poor needing a night's lodging; the old cemetery with its polychrome tombstones—no sign of any of them.

Yet destruction had not reached the houses beyond Jewish Kazimierz on the other side of the River Grodarz. In my youthful fantasies these had represented the outside world. They included the former post office where my heart used to pound while I waited for the mailman, because his scuffed leather pouch might contain the reactions to my early literary efforts. My hopes were realized one wintry afternoon, for he handed me a magazine which had published my first poem, "Golden Polish Autumns."

From the post office the road led to Plebania Street. The high fortress-like walls of the Paulist monastery extended to the right; to the left, the large villa and estate of the Ulanowskis, and the junior high school where Sonia Szenderowicz-Wisnia had devotedly guided us along the path of secular knowledge. The courtyard was deserted but unchanged. The great platform that had served as a stage for school performances was still there. One of our big events had been the staging of Slowacki's symbolist tragedy, *Balladyna*, in which I took the leading role of Kirkor, a knight dressed in golden armor and white eagles' wings. His speech rebuking the evil Polish prince Popiel broke out of the deep recesses of my memory.

> *Oh, anarchy, worse then the plagues of Moses,*
> *Dirties our earth and spreads ever farther.*
> *That same Poland of harvests and plenty*
> *Is turned to a granary swarming with locusts.*

Driven by a sudden impulse, I climbed up to the magnificent park. I had experienced my first romantic tremors among its wide-branching oaks and slim birches. The forest's bare trees seemed shrunken now, and the old oaks were gone. Blades of green grass were peeking out on the meadow from which the wind had blown the dry snow. I saw coming toward me the owner of the estate, Tadeusz Ulanowski, whose tall figure had grown slightly stooped.

The stern, almost angry expression on his bony, smoothly shaven face was suddenly transformed into pleased surprise. He had evidently recognized me, and began to stride faster, amiably waving his knobby brown cane. I remembered this cane for its silver handle, molded in the shape of a woman's head. Ulanowski used to have it tucked coquettishly under his arm. Jealousy and resentment took hold of me: this walking stick had survived Jewish Kazimierz.

"Very nice of you to visit us. We heard that you were here. My wife will be very pleased to see you," Ulanowski said, holding onto my hand. Like Pisula, he asked who in my family had survived. A descendant of an old patrician family that had always maintained friendly relations with Jews, Ulanowski had been the mayor of Kazimierz when World War II broke out, and had kept the post throughout the Nazi Occupation. According to the testimony of the few Jews who had survived, Ulanowski had done everything possible to ease the Jews' bitter lot. He had acted as intermediary between the *Judenrat* and the Nazi commandant, Ghede, who had offered to delay the first deportation from the ghetto for a pound of gold. Ghede had taken the gold, but carried out the selection a few days later anyway.

In Ulanowski's house there were landscapes of Kazimierz painted by the noted Jewish artist, Natan Korzen. One picture immortalized a vanished fragment of Jewish life in the *shtetl*—the butchers' stores behind the synagogue on market day, with Jews and peasants milling among the horses and cattle. As I looked at this painting, Mrs. Ulanowski told me that Korzen, who had stayed with them every summer for many years, had remained late into the autumn the season of 1939. When rumors spread that a ghetto would be set up in Kazimierz, he had gone back to Warsaw. For a time the Ulanowskis had continued to receive letters from him; then all contact had ceased.

The meeting with the Ulanowskis was a sad experience for me. They were witnesses who did not claim, as some others did, to have risked their lives for Jews, and honestly discussed the agonizing years of Nazi rule.

"Our country was cursed; it became the graveyard of the Jews," Ulanowski said. He decided to resign his post several times, only to be dissuaded by the chairman of the *Judenrat*, Chaim Feuerstein.

As he looked back at the harrowing past, Ulanowski said he had concluded that the population of Kazimierz had not behaved as it should and could have. He felt that the younger Jews, particularly the women who could possibly have passed for Poles, might have been hidden by the townspeople. But until the deportations actually began, Ulanowski added—they occurred later there than in all the surrounding towns—he had nursed the illusion that in Kazimierz the Jews would survive the war. I said nothing when he observed that he and his friends had been puzzled by the silence of the outside world. To them it had been an indication that the Allies were indifferent to the fate of the Jews in Poland.

As we parted, I asked the former mayor of Kazimierz whether he knew anything about the holy vessels of the ancient synagogue, particularly the ark-curtain embroidered by Esther. Ulanowski explained that the Rabbi of Kazimierz, Israel Zilberminc, had taken these holy articles with him when the last transport of Jews left the ghetto.

★ ★ ★ ★ ★

As long as I can remember, I have never cried while alone, not even in moments of deep despair. But on this first evening after my arrival in Kazimierz, I wept. I had been wandering through the streets and squares of the town for hours. When I entered the room assigned to me in the House of the Architects, I broke down.

The hostel itself added to my sadness. The Union of Polish Architects had built it on the site of three destroyed Jewish houses which had belonged to the Honigbaum, Kornberg and Zamoiski families. It was intended as a center where artists, writers and other intellectuals could work and rest.

That night, from my window, I saw several carloads of cheerful young people come down the road from Pulawy to spend the weekend in the House of the Architects. The marketplace was brightly lit by blazing lights, but my memory evoked Sabbath candles flickering in their brass and silver candleholders.

Early that Saturday morning, I was awakened by the tolling of the three church bells, all different in pitch and volume. First came the heavy, awesome peal from the church on the southern end of town; then from the north, the two-toned chime of the main church, the Fara; and, finally in the east, the thin, childlike tinkle from the

Church of Saint Anne on Lublin Street. Behind the Mountain of the Three Crosses the rising sun made the sky glow.

Soon afterwards Berek Cytrin knocked at my door. He was the only Jew who had remained in Kazimierz. I knew that he lived in Pulawy under the assumed name of Boleslaw Zielinski. During the Nazi Occupation, he had been hidden by a peasant family in the village of Bochotnica, where his uncle, Ezekiel Fried, had owned a mill. When Cytrin came out of hiding, he found that everything but the mill's wheel had been carried off; and that the mansion of his large, ramified family, most of whom had perished, was occupied by peasants from nearby villages.

Cytrin threw himself into my arms, his rugged face tense with pent-up emotion. After a long silence, he broke into sobs. It was as if he were releasing a deeply repressed lament that had been mounting in him for years.

I knew him from his childhood. He had been brought to Kazimierz to live with a relative after his parents were murdered by bandits in the neighboring village of Karczmisk. In his earthy Polish interspersed with typical peasant expressions and Jewish sighs, he told me how he had survived the war. He had spent the entire four years alone in a pigsty hidden from the Nazis as well as the peasants he had known since he was a boy. From his hiding place he had often seen young hooligans searching in the barn, rummaging through the potato cellars. He had even heard them discussing the hidden Jew, for whose head the Nazis would give the magnificent reward of a few pounds of sugar. There was a flash of ironic understanding in Berek Cytrin's observation that his hunters felt no hatred for him; they simply considered him a "fox to be skinned for its pelt."

He spoke highly of the peasant who had hidden him throughout the Occupation at the risk of his family's life as well as his own.

"How can I leave now?" Cytrin asked, as if he needed to justify himself. He revealed the inner turmoil of lonely Jews in the dead *shtetlekh* of Poland, married to the gentile women who had saved them. He went on to stress that his devoted wife, the daughter of the man who had saved him, and his two daughters considered themselves Jewish, and were ready to leave Poland with him at a moment's notice.

Cytrin stayed with me all day, accompanying me to my meeting with the architect, Karol Sicinsky, who was curator of historic Kazimierz. In his spacious studio on Senatorska Street in the restored Renaissance building of the Celejow family, I saw fragments of polychrome tombstones from the old cemetery. There were prayer books on a shelf, almanacs, brass candlesticks, and Hanukah lamps, that had been unearthed in some basement. Sicinski also showed us two drawings by the famous Polish painter, Waclaw Wąsowicz, depicting crowds of Jews in the marketplace during the last deportation to Belzec. Wąsowicz had drawn these from the window of the town hall. An act of heroism, Sicinski thought.

He assured me that he was gathering together all the Jewish memorabilia he could find for the proposed town museum, and hinted that he expected financial assistance for this project from the surviving Kazimierz Jews now scattered throughout the world.

After my conversation with the custodian of this 700-year-old Jewish community's mementos, it became obvious that there was no place in Kazimierz for a living Jew. This was re-affirmed for me by Berek Cytrin for, as we strolled through the streets and courtyards of the *shtetl*, he shared my uneasiness at the hostile looks being levelled at us.

When the war ended, Berek Cytrin-Zielinski had tried to resettle in Kazimierz, but his best Polish friends, particularly the Ulanowskis in whose house he had grown up, had dissuaded him from doing so. They simply feared for his life, since neither the older nor the new Polish inhabitants wanted anyone to remind them of the murdered Jews whose homes, possessions and even clothes they had grabbed.

4

THE LAST HEBREW LETTERS

"I have set the Lord always before me . . ."

Carved into a heavy oaken beam, the Hebrew letters are the only reminder of a Jewish community that flourished in Kazimierz for seven centuries.

They were discovered in a massive stone house fronting on the marketplace of the old *shtetl* — the quotation from the Book of Psalms (16:8) that adorns the Ark of every synagogue. The normally square Hebrew characters are modified by a style which points to their late medieval or early Renaissance origin. They hover above the crowned heads of two human-faced lions and other fragments of traditional ornamentation, all chiseled into the same beam. At some time in the past, this fortress-like building must have been a house of worship.

There is no mention of it in the legends about Kazimierz, which date back to the chronicles of Jan Dlugosz, the earliest recorder of Poland's history. No documentary evidence indicates that there was ever a synagogue in the town's marketplace near the Przybylo brothers' houses, whose facades are decorated with the reliefs of saints.

The merchant Aaron Lustig, who last owned the house containing the Hebrew inscription, was unaware that the roof over his family's head had centuries earlier looked down upon his ancestors at prayer. It was not until the spring of 1940, when the Nazis had herded the Jews of Kazimierz into a ghetto on the outskirts of the *shtetl* and peasants from a neighboring village had moved into Lustig's house, that the sacred lettering reappeared under the layers of peeling paint.

Famed throughout Poland, the Synagogue of Kazimierz stood on a side street behind the marketplace. According to legend, it was built in the 14th century by King Kazimierz the Great as a tender gift to his Jewish mistress Esther. Some of its stones were reputed to have come from the Wailing Wall itself, brought from Jerusalem by pilgrims, traders or Crusaders. Miraculously untouched by bombardments, the Great Synagogue lasted until the final days of World War II. Before the Nazis left the town they wrecked the synagogue and desecrated the altar. Afterwards vandals from neighboring villages ripped out the benches and patinated lecterns, whose decorative carvings had preserved the names of generations of worshipppers. They also tore down the lofty, eight-panelled ceiling, covered with fantastic wildlife paintings—deer, rams, lions, fish, eagles—as well as scenes of the Holy Land such as Rachel's Tomb and the Wailing Wall. When the orgy of destruction was over, only the bare stone walls of the Great Synagogue remained.

Also obliterated was the historic Jewish cemetery at the end of Lublin Road, dominated by the huge mausoleum of the Wonder-Rebbe Ezekiel Taub, founder of the Kazimierz Hasidic dynasty. The multihued tombstones and sarcophagi of the Jewish patricians—the grain and timber merchants who had earned for the town its reputation as "little Danzig"—these were stolen and a number of them used to pave the courtyard of Kazimierz's medieval Paulist monastery.

Thus, the last vestiges of this ancient Jewish community were wiped out shortly after the liberation. The Hebrew letters that had emerged on the house in the marketplace seemed a contemporary version of *mene mene tekel upharsin* (Daniel 5:25), the writing on the wall—without a Daniel to interpret the warning.

The man responsible for the physical restoration of Kazimierz, the architect and art historian, Karol Sicinski, had for years waged a lone battle against the neglect of Jewish landmarks along both banks of the Vistula. Acting as my guide, Sicinski was particularly proud of his "archeological find" in Aaron Lustig's house: the Hebrew quotation and Renaissance carvings. He believed that the beam hailed from the oldest Jewish house of prayer in Kazimierz, probably constructed in the late 14th or very early 15th century, when it had already become a bustling commercial center on the Cracow-Danzig waterway. The tolerance of early Catholic kings, who had encouraged Jewish settlement in Poland, was already then giving way to discrimination. Nevertheless, the Jews of Kazimierz played a prominent role in their town's developing commerce. The synagogue, linked stubbornly to the Esther legend, was to be built centuries later. Its location on a side street rather than in the market square indicated that the privileges once granted Jewish residents of Polish cities had been withdrawn.

Sicinski took me to see the beam which had been cleansed at his insistence. As we entered the building, he was embarrassed to find its occupant butchering a freshly-slaughtered pig. The carcass was laid out on a long table near a window and a barrel filled with boiling water; steam was still rising from the hide. On the wall above hung a faded color print of the Madonna, her sad troubled eyes looking across the room toward the Hebrew letters on the polished oak beam.

The other traces of the once glorious Jewish community were buried in the town hall's archives, next to the house of Aaron Lustig. The secretary of the town hall, Jan Peplowski, showed me the ledger listing the births of all Kazimierz Jews as far back as the 17th century. After Poland's partition at the end of the 18th century, entries were made in Russian. It was a heavy volume of thick, ash-gray pages, bound in yellowing, nearly transparent parchment; as I turned those pages, I found many familiar names, including those of my family and my own. The earliest entries had become illegible; faded by time, they were faint, rosy shadows.

Scholars have never been able to unravel myth from fact in the historical fabric of Kazimierz, nor to distinguish between Polish and Jewish history. The two have fused ever since Kazimierz began as a small settlement, long before King Kazimierz gave it his name.

To this day the majestic ruins of the castle stand on the highest spot in Kazimierz, their limestone walls glistening gold in the summer sunlight and reflecting the blue-white of winter snow. A tall stone tower, called the Baszta, which rises on an adjoining hill, was a lighthouse for the river traffic in the days when Kazimierz was a busy port. Legend tells that a tunnel connected the lighthouse with the castle of Esther in nearby Bochotnica, where she stayed when her beloved lord attended to matters of state in Cracow, or led his army into battle against Poland's enemies. She spent the lonely days embroidering a golden curtain intended for the Ark of the town's synagogue. The Jews of Kazimierz handed the Esther legend from one generation to the next, and firmly believed that this very curtain had lasted through the centuries. They were sure that it had survived the fires that frequently razed their wooden houses of worship before the Great Synagogue was erected in stone during the early part of the 18th century. The curtain's dominant motif was a fantasy-like creature breathing fire. It was thought to be the serpent that tempted Eve in Paradise. And, indeed, this conjecture suited the romanticism of the Esther story.

An eminent historian and expert in Polish art, Waclaw Husarski, who has written an exhaustive monograph on Kazimierz, asserts that the curtain was "an import from China," made in the second half of the 18th century when Chinese art and handicrafts were highly fashionable in Europe. I remember often gazing at this curtain; for me it had the characteristics of a Chinese dragon. As I matured, I could clearly discern the difference between the hues of the serpent's golden thread and those of the crowns and arabesques embroidered at the top.

The Ark hanging was used only during the High Holy Days and on special occasions. Members of the Chevra Kadisha, the town's burial society, would then guard the synagogue day and night. The rest of the year the curtain was stored for safe-keeping along with other precious vessels in a vault at the home of Vovtche Bromberg, a man who gave the appearance of wealth long after he had lost it,

The author's birthplace: the Danzig House in Kazimierz, in which his family lived for generations.

when his transactions with the timber dealers of Danzig had ceased. Moderately tall and broad-shouldered, he always kept his graying, once-auburn beard neatly trimmed. Even on weekdays he wore a long, black silk caftan, though it had become somewhat threadbare and faded. A heavy gold watch chain dangling from his green velvet vest, he would stroll through the marketplace, poised and dignified, offering old friends a pinch of snuff from a small box of engraved gold studded with precious stones.

In the days of my youth, Bromberg was still part owner of Danzig House, the biggest building in the town's market square. The huge stone structure had cellars deep and large enough to provide shelter in time of war for half of the towns' Jewish population. Its carriage house still contained gaily painted wheels and leather harnesses, left over from the horse-drawn carriages the Bromberg family had used in their travels. The only three-story building in Kazimierz, its facade bore the date 1554, without the "A.D." found on the houses of the Christian nobility. It had obviously been built by a Jew, in all likelihood a merchant engaged in the Danzig trade. Its architecture, its heavy escarpments and wrought-iron balconies clearly imitated the mansions of that great Baltic port, where the Vistula enters the sea.

Vovtche Bromberg's spacious personal apartment, with its tremendous drawing room, sitting rooms and bedrooms, was often the setting for wedding parties of leading Jewish families and receptions were held there for prominent visitors from out of town, Jewish and non-Jewish alike. One tale of the glories in the Bromberg family's heyday told of a wedding celebrated at the turn of the century. Hundreds of guests came from every part of Poland, and a famous Jewish chef, specially brought in from Danzig, created a marvelous dish with the bride's white leather glove chopped into it; since it constituted less than a sixtieth of the ingredients, his culinary creation was deemed kosher according to Jewish dietary laws.

Another sign of the Brombergs' great wealth was their permanent *succah*. Most families put up a temporary structure in their yard for the eight days of the autumnal Feast of Tabernacles. The Brombergs' *succah* was an integral part of their home. An ingenious device in the attic rolled away a section of the roof to meet the requirement that a *succah* be open to the sky. It had been decorated by the celebrated artist, Abraham Shiffman, when he came from nearby Lublin in the 1890's to restore the ceiling paintings of the Great Synagogue, and to add a large new fresco to its Eastern wall. He painted a triptych for the Brombergs' depicting the life of the Israelites after the Exodus from Egypt as they wandered through the desert, living in tents and observing the Feast of Tabernacles there.

An attraction for tourists who flocked to Kazimierz every summer from all corners of Poland was a visit to the room in the Bromberg home where Queen Esther's curtain and the silver and gold vessels belonging to the Great Synagogue were displayed. There was also a prayer book commemorating the disaster that befell the Jewish community of Kazimierz after the Swedish-Polish war in 1656, when the cavalrymen of Hetman Stefan Czarnecki celebrated a victory over the Swedes with a pogrom in Kazimierz, an orgy of murder and looting that devastated the stores and homes of its Jewish merchants.

The names of the 72 men, women and children slain in cold blood were inscribed in this prayer book, and each winter a memorial service was held in the Great Synagogue on the anniversary of their death. The cantor would sing *El Molai Rahamim*, the traditional chant for the dead, and the president of the community read out the list of martyrs. In my child's mind that day was a second *Tisha b'Av* (Ninth of the month of Av), the day of mourning for the destroyed Second Temple in Jerusalem.

The prayer book, holy curtain and sacred vessels all vanished during the Nazi occupation.

5

THE RENAISSANCE TOWN

The earliest documentary record about Kazimierz goes back to the year 1008. King Boleslaw Chrobry (the Valiant), the famous conqueror of the city of Kiev, made a gift of a small village on the Vistula to some Benedictine monks. It was then known as Wietrzna Gora. Three centuries later, 23-year-old King Kazimierz the Great bought the village back from the Order, proclaimed it a city, and built a summer palace on a plateau that dominated the area.

The tiny community developed rapidly into an important center of commerce. Trading caravans began coming to Kazimierz from the neighboring lands of Prussia and Russia, and across greater distances from Sweden and Italy. The first Jewish merchants and craftsmen arrived, and found Poland a haven from the persecutions they had suffered in the ghettos of Germany.

The most significant document expressing medieval Poland's tolerance toward Jews was the Statute of Kalisz, issued in 1264 by Boleslaw the Pious, Duke of Kalisz. Especially meaningful for Jews was the Biblical language of the Statute, which began with the phrase, "In the name of God, Amen". Moreover, it contained 36 paragraphs, twice the mystical number 18, that also spells *chai* (life) in Hebrew.

In 1334, a year after he ascended the throne of Poland, King Kazimierz issued a proclamation substantially broadening the privileges granted to Jews, whose favored status during his reign from 1333-1370 was of particular benefit to the community in Kazimierz. The admiration and affection they bore him was expressed in century-old romantic legends about the king's love for the Jewess Esther.

Poland's historians have differed about the authenticity of these tales. Some have seen them as mere paraphrases of the Biblical story about Queen Esther and King Ahasuerus, stimulated by the friendliness which Kazimierz demonstrated toward the Jews. Others have cited them as proof of the humaneness of a great ruler toward a persecuted people. Yet others regarded them as insults to a good Catholic king. It would be difficult to determine whether the seemingly scholarly attempts to present the Esther story as pure fancy or fiction were dictated by ignorance, or by anti-Semitic tendencies to deny any role Jews played in early Polish history. However, the facts that have subsequently emerged could not be suppressed or eradicated. In the 18th century, Tadeusz Czacki, a liberal historian, courageously opposed the efforts of his colleagues to eradicate all mention of Esther from the life of King Kazimierz the Great. He was one of the first Polish thinkers to offer a fair evaluation of the contributions that Jews had made to the nation's development and maintained that he had even seen a portrait of Esther, painted by an Italian artist in the court of King Kazimierz. However, the portrait mysteriously disappeared and no other historian has mentioned it.

Later historians have tended to dismiss the story of Esther as of little significance — the conclusion also of Waclaw Husarski, who spent a lifetime researching the history of Kazimierz, and whose monograph was awarded a prize by the Polish communist regime, when it was published in 1953, shortly after his death. There is no way of knowing whether his manuscript was doctored by the Stalinist censors. But the scant attention it pays to the role that Jews have played during the reign of King Kazimierz is in line with the trend of communist historians to minimize the contribution of the Jewish community during the thousand-year history of Poland. The monograph makes no reference at all to the persecutions the Jews of Kazimierz endured during periods of repression. It does not even allude to the prayer book mentioned above, listing the victims of the 17th-century pogrom, though Husarski certainly knew of its existence, since he must have been present at the annual memorial services for these martyrs. While his exposition contains many valuable and previously unknown facts about Kazimierz, he sneers at the legends about Esther and the king; a "loving couple cooing against a background of colorful landscapes and magnificent medieval palaces. He, the king, the powerful ruler. She, the daughter of a persecuted nation. How enchanting, romantic, sentimental! . . . The whole story is sheer fantasy, none too skillfully embroidered on a background of skimpy historic fact."

Husarski speaks of his discovery of documents showing that Jews lived in the town at the beginning of the 16th century, and "probably much earlier." As evidence of the size and affluence of the Jewish community during that period, he quotes a request for permission to build a stone synagogue after their wooden one had been destroyed by fire.

In addition to being traders, Jews in 16th-century Kazimierz were practitioners of the brewer's art, which they developed to a degree unknown in Poland. A chronicle in the year 1545 records that the brewers of Kazimierz were producing the equivalent of four million litres of beer annually, selling their output throughout the Lublin province, in Polish Pomerania and in the port of Danzig.

The grain trade also had a strong influence on the town's growth. Its Renaissance granaries stored the crops yielded by the fertile fields of the region for shipment down the Vistula to Danzig. In 1588, sixteen per cent of Poland's total grain exports moved through Kazimierz. The international grain merchants of Italy, Britain and the Netherlands, Greece and Sweden had buyers in Kazimierz, many of whom settled there. In time their names were polonized, but evidences of their foreign origin can still be found in the town: some of the houses built by Italians have Latin quotations from Seneca inscribed on their facades.

At some point during the late 15th or early 16th century, Kazi-mierz's market day, which had drawn traders from all over the region for hundreds of years, was changed from Saturday to Tues-day, obviously at the insistence of Jewish merchants; it has remained Tuesday to this day.

For more than 400 years the marketplace hummed weekly like a beehive, as buyers and sellers were active from dawn to dusk. The town square and the streets leading to it were filled with peasants' wagons bringing fruit and vegetables to be piled high on vendors' stands or on the ground. Deals between the merchants and peas-ants were closed with much backslapping, handshaking and drink-ing and quacking ducks, hissing geese, and cackling chickens added to the noise. There was lively trading in cattle and horses near a row of wooden stalls with thatched roofs and brightly painted doors, occupied by kosher butchers. Jewish artisans and merchants came from nearby villages on both banks of the river to offer their wares—poultry and other foods, yard goods and cloth-ing, utensils, pots and pans. Pottery was recognized as a specialty of the Jews.

By the first half of the 17th century Kazimierz, reputed to be one of the wealthiest and most beautiful towns in Poland, had 280 stone houses, and a population of more than 3,000, making it a fair-sized center by the standards of the time.

There are no precise figures on the Jewish population. All histo-rians of the period agree that it was substantial, and Husarski makes the snide observation that it was "large enough." The whole province of Lublin had some 8,000 people.

The prosperity of the Jewish community in Kazimierz aroused jealousy among the town's Polish inhabitants, who petitioned the king to limit their privileges and to place economic restraints on them. Husarski reports: "There was a law on the books forbidding Jews to live on the market square and, in 1645, King Wladyslaw IV ordered confiscation of the home belonging to the Jew Levos." He also states that in 1766 the Rector of the Church school, Monsignor Franciszek Wolski, charged the Jews with "violating the regula-tions of Christian towns . . . . They are pushing themselves into the marketplace where they buy and rent houses."

In the 16th and 17th centuries, when Kazimierz was one of Poland's flourishing centers, prominent members of the aristocracy—the Czartoryskis, the Lubomirskis and Radziwills—were frequent visitors, especially in the summer, leasing their granaries and river boats to Jews with whom they engaged in grain and timber trade.

Among the eminent visitors to the town were the 16th century poets, Mikolaj Rej and Jan Kochanowski, who are regarded as the fathers of Polish literature. In none of their works is there the slightest mention of Jews, in Kazimierz or elsewhere in Poland—an omission especially puzzling in the case of Kochanowski, whose loving and masterful translation of the Psalms of David is one of the classics of Polish poetry. He came from Czarnolas, a huge estate close to the *shtetl* of Zvolin, named after the dark forests of tall firs surrounding it on the Vistula bank opposite Kazimierz. He had many links with the town and his daughter married one of its wealthy landowners, Mikolaj Borkowski. In 1580, Kochanowski was the presiding judge at a murder trial in Kazimierz that grew out of a scandalous love affair involving two noble Polish families.

Among the leading families of Kazimierz mentioned in the town records are the Przybylo brothers, the Lenards, the Bartons, the Firlejs and the Celejows, who were descendants of Italian nobility. A Gomulka is also named among the town's Polish patricians, although there is no evidence that he made any valuable contribution to its growth. Having listed the local aristocracy at the end of the 15th century, Husarski adds:

"There was also a number of important Jews in the town. Property deeds carry the names of such influential Jewish families as Yelen, Davidovicz, and Moszek Jozwowicz. They succeeded the Przybylo brothers as lessees of the collection of taxes, the office for weights and measures, the concessions for the milling of flour, and the production of beer and other alcoholic beverages. After Moszek Jozwowicz died, the lease passed to his widow, Frumet."

Jewish names such as Philip Lack, Daniel Falcowicz, David Wilham, Jakub Rabenicz, appear in municipal documents with the notation: "Merchant from Danzig." There is also mention of an architect, Jakub Ballin who, between 1610 and 1613, restored the great Renaissance church, the "Phara," which had been gutted by fire. Ecclesiastical records list him as a resident of Lublin, originally from Venice, information based on the wording of a plaque for many years affixed to the church wall, which disappeared during a subsequent restoration. Was Jakub Ballin a Jew? There is no specific evidence, but it is known that a branch of the famous Ballin family of Venice settled in Germany, for a scion of that ancient Jewish line, Albert Ballin, was the founder of her modern merchant marine.

Kazimierz knew war and invasion frequently. Its reputation as a thriving commercial center with rich warehouses and granaries attracted greedy commanders of invading armies. In 1648, the Cossacks of the fierce Ukrainian, Hetman Bogdan Chmielnicki, who took Kazimierz, were driven out by Polish forces, but not before they had carried out pogroms against the Jewish population.

6

JEWISH PATRICIANS

For five hundred years the Jews of Kazimierz fought for the right to own homes in the marketplace. This "privilege" was frequently withdrawn and then returned by various Polish monarchs.

In 1787, the last Polish king, Stanislaw August Poniatowski, personally intervened in the feud between Jewish and Polish merchants in the town. He restricted the right of Jews to live on the marketplace and to lease granaries and ships from Polish magnates who did business with them. Jews were active in the grain trade of Kazimierz at that time. Samuel Jakubowicz Zbytkover, an elder of the Praga community and one of the richest Jews in Poland, who had his granaries there and owned a number of towns and villages around Warsaw, was appointed in 1776, by King Stanislaw August as grain supplier to his court. Zbytkover soon found himself in a dilemma, caught between his loyalty to the king and the pressures of the pro-Russian magnates of the "Targowica"* conspiracy—the

---

* To Polish patriots the town "Targowica" had become synonymous with treason, because the conspiracy hatched there led to the second partition of Poland in 1792.

Potockis, the Sapiehas, and the Branickis—whose granaries and ships he was leasing.

The partition of Poland curtailed trade between east and west, and led to the decline of Kazimerz. At the beginning of the 19th century, its entire grain trade passed into the hands of Jews, and its population became almost entirely Jewish. Polish historians mention this with bitterness. Husarski quotes a sermon of the priest, Woronicz, which compared the ruin of Kazimierz with the destruction of Jerusalem by paraphrasing the lament of the Prophet Jeremiah.

The 1834 annual Warsaw almanac, called *Jutrzenka* (Dawn), opens with an engraving of the Kazimierz panorama, showing the ruins of the royal palace. A lengthy account follows of the town's glorious past and subsequent demise. It reached the point where "the overwhelming majority of the population which totals 1800 souls consists of Israelites. As a result, the town isn't particularly distinguished for its cleanliness. . . . The Christians work the land. The hills around the city are bedecked with orchards, and their dried plums and the jam made in Kazimierz are famous throughout the region."

The author fails to mention that the renowned apple and plum orchards were operated by Jews, and that it was they who revived the grain trade with Danzig after the standstill that followed the partition of Poland.

An etching by Adolf Teben, dated 1844, bears witness to the role Jews played in the grain trade with foreign countries during the first half of the 19th century. It depicts a scene at the Danzig grain exchange where some twenty-odd men pose in the fashionable dress of the day—tall hats, short coats and pointed shoes. Several among them hold bowls filled with kernels, samples of the barley, wheat and oats being offered for sale. On this engraving the massive figure of Meyer Wolf Feuerstein is conspicuous for its beard; the other men wear only sideburns. Some of the names listed in the caption suggest Jewish origins: Isaac Goldstein, I. L. Yoel, P. Zaltzman, Lazar Goldschmidt, Samuel Baum, and Hirsh Levin, and Feuerstein's name is followed by the words, "from Kazimierz," indicating that he was the only merchant there representing Poland. Until the outbreak of World War II this etching hung in the

The Feuerstein Granary in Kazimierz.

house of the Feuerstein family, who owned the last two stone granaries dating back to the 14th and 15th centuries. Feuerstein's grandchildren later converted them into a tannery and a sawmill, which survive to this day, and have been nationalized by the fledgling Polish People's Republic. The author of the Nationalization Act of 1945 and first Minister for National Economy, Hilary Minc, was a descendant of the Feuersteins; his mother, Stefanie, had grown up in Kazimierz.

Not a single Feuerstein returned to the town after the Liberation. The family records have disappeared, among them the priceless documents describing the financial assistance they gave to the Polish insurrectionists, as well as the Danzig engraving that had once hung in Maurice Feuerstein's living room. Perhaps the only other copy of it has been preserved in New York by Menahem Mendl Feuerstein, who until Hitler came to power, lived in Danzig, where he owned a large grain business, and was a member of the grain exchange. The original of the engraving featuring his great-grandfather may still be seen in the Danzig Chamber of Commerce.

Many stories were told in Kazimierz about Meyer Wolf Feuerstein's wealth and his philanthropic endeavors. He was remembered especially for helping to build a court for the hasidic Rebbe, Ezekiel Taub, a disciple of Yaakov Yitzhak Halevi of Lublin, "the Seer." Thus he helped lay the foundation for the great hasidic dynasty in Kazimierz. One remarkable, frequently retold episode involving Meyer Wolf Feuerstein demonstrates the extent of his wealth as well as his indifference to it. On a dark night in the late autumn of 1830, a courier rode into town, rapped on the shutters of the first large house on the marketplace, and asked where Feuerstein lived. Since it was a period of mounting Polish opposition to czarist rule, culminating in the tragic November Uprising, the runner's arrival shook the entire town, and the Jews gathered in the courtyard outside the house to learn what news the mysterious messenger had brought. After a long wait, Meyer Wolf Feuerstein came out on his porch and calmly informed the crowd that the courier had merely brought news that his transport of timber and grain had gone down during a storm on the Vistula. The loss was estimated at two hundred thousand thalers—a huge sum in those days—but Feuerstein shrugged it off and told the people to go home to sleep, so that they could get up in time for morning services. At daybreak, he came to the house of prayer as if nothing had happened.

In that 1830-1831 uprising, the mountains and valleys around the town and its marketplace were the scene of one of the bloodiest battles, which took place on April 18, 1831, on the road between Kazimierz and Wąwolnice, since then called Czerniawy, "the black tempest." Though it is not known whether the Jews of Kazimierz fought in the campaign led by the Polish general, Jan Conti-Julian Sierawski, it is established that the Feuersteins and other Jewish merchants supported the uprising financially, and supplied provisions to General Sierawski's forces, later defeated near Korow. But in the numerous monographs written about Kazimierz, there is no mention of the help that the town's Jews gave to that uprising. On the other hand, the latest handbook, by Lech Pietrzak, published in 1957, states that, during the later Uprising of 1863, the town's Jewish community gave "160 pairs of boots and as many sheepskins" to the cavalry detachments of General Walerian Wroblewski*, who won a victory over the Czar's Cossacks between Kazimierz and Bochotnica. In a letter to the Jewish community he expressed his thanks for the gracious manner in which it had welcomed his troops. The czarist authorities punished the town's patriots for this act, demoting it to the status of an *osada*, a settlement.

My own family preserved a treasured document written in Polish and brought from neighboring Wąwolnice to Kazimierz by my maternal grandfather, Mordecai Mandelbaum—a long, thick sheet of yellowed parchment with a brown wax seal, which was confirmation by the quartermaster of Count Malachowski's regiment that Mordecai Mandelbaum had contributed oxen, horses, provisions, and money for its use. The young count fell in the battle and was buried near the town on the Czerniawy heights. The stone tablet on his grave still bears the epitaph: "Juliusz, Count Malachowski, born 1802, fell on this spot on April 18, 1831."

---

* In 1871 Wroblewski fought on the barricades of the Paris Commune.

During the czarist regime, the Malachowski document was hidden in the cellar of our house. My family also possessed memorabilia that were camouflaged symbols of Jewish-Polish patriotism. In the credenza in our dining room, which held the family silverware and some old amber pipes, there were two large, gilt-edged porcelain plates, used only during Passover, on which symbolic religious embellishments camouflaged the forbidden crowned Polish eagles. These could be detected easily if one knew just how to turn the plates.

A Polish eagle, made of white beads and capped with a crown embroidered in gold thread, was also concealed behind a round piece of red velvet sewn onto a pin cushion. When Poland's independence was declared in 1918, my grandmother ceremoniously unstitched the velvet to reveal the white eagle and the gold crown. Tourists who visited the Bromberg house to see Esther's holy curtain and other relics, often stopped at our home to see the pincushion and the plates.

7

REB EZEKIEL OF KUZMIR

During the first half of the 19th century, when czarist oppression
in Poland reached new dimensions, Kazimierz became an important hasidic center with its own philosophy. Thousands of disciples
from all parts of the country streamed into the town to seek conso-
lation from Reb Ezekiel Taub, who, although he stemmed from
Plonsk, soon became known as Reb Ezekiel of Kuzmir (the Yiddish name for Kazimierz).

The bountiful landscape, its lush gardens and orchards on the
banks of the Vistula and the enveloping hills, provided an ideal
background for the way of life preached by Reb Ezekiel. In those
uneasy times when Jews were greatly troubled, he taught that
solace and exaltation could best be attained through song. He had
inherited his musical inclinations from his father, Reb Zvi Hirsh,
who, though a businessman, was known in Plonsk as a singer and
composer of Sabbath and Holy Day chants. He sent his gifted son
to the Lublin *tzadik**, Yaakov Yitzhak Halevi Horovitz known as

---

* A righteous man.

the *Chozeh* ("the Seer"), and leader of the hasidic movement in Greater Poland. As soon as young Ezekiel set foot in the Rebbe's house of prayer in Lublin, the worshippers nicknamed him "The Tall Plonsker." Yet he was greatly respected on account of his family, for his grandfather, Reb Solomon of Raciąz, had been a disciple of the Baal Shem Tov, founder of the hasidic movement.

When the Seer died in 1815, his most prominent Hasidim invited his closest disciples to set up courts in their towns. The Tall Plonsker settled in Ciepilew, near Ilza, but he was quickly driven out of town by the non-hasidic Jews, even though he had distinguished himself by his wisdom and his singing, because they had become alarmed at the rising cost of living caused by the influx of the Hasidim. Reb Ezekiel then settled in Kazimierz, where the wealthy grain and timber merchants, the Feuersteins in particular, maintained him in grand style. Like the Seer before him, Reb Ezekiel kept a court jester, who played the role of a bogus *rebbe* and even responded to ritual questions. At one Purim festivity he overstepped all bounds and mocked Reb Ezekiel with the observation that had he, the jester, *not* been so well versed in the Holy Scriptures, he too might have become a Rebbe. This was an obvious slur upon Reb Ezekiel, who devoted more time to chanting than to studying.

Chaim Minc, a tycoon and an in-law of the Feuersteins, was a constant source of tales about the conduct and miracles of Reb Ezekiel. To the end of his days, Minc strolled through town wearing a flame-colored Turkish robe and white skullcap which used to sink into the mop of bushy gray hair that merged with his flowing beard, and smoked a long, amber-stemmed pipe until the last moment of his 105-year-old life. The venerable old man related how despite the snowy January weather, the funeral of Reb Ezekiel drew thousands of Hasidim from all corners of Poland who escorted the corpse of the *tzadik* to its final resting place with chants that he himself had composed.

According to Chaim Minc's description, Reb Ezekiel was an unusually tall man, as could be seen from his gabardines, his long, gnarled cane with its silver handle, and the high carved lectern from which he preached—memorabilia preserved in the Rebbe's personal sanctum of the hasidic court where several families of his descendants lived until the Nazis invaded Kazimierz. He had performed his miracles with a cane that reached the top of the average man's head; he exorcized dybbuks and drove out demons that plagued local artisans; these evil spirits, according to legend, snipped off the tips of boots at the shoemakers'; they also smashed the earthenware pots containing *cholent*, the traditional Sabbath dish kept heated all night in bakery ovens.

With this very cane the Rebbe even stopped the flow of the Grodarz, the skimpy local stream. All year long it trickled by lazily, but when the snow on nearby mountains melted in the spring, it turned into a raging torrent that demolished bridges connecting both sides of the town, carrying off scores of wooden houses and stables. The Rebbe's cane, lectern and gabardines contrasted sharply with the short bed in which he slept bent double. Nearby stood a tall wooden armchair, and on the bare oak table was a pair of pewter candlesticks.

Chaim Minc also described a custom introduced by the Rebbe: when the three church-bells rang daily at dawn and at sunset, causing apprehension among the Jews, Reb Ezekiel and his disciples responded by chanting. For generations the Jews of Kazimierz sang the hymns and repeated the wisdom of Reb Ezekiel who preached meekness. But when it came to divine services, he contended that they must be conducted with animation and joy, *lebedig un lustig* were his words in Yiddish. As an instance of this, a story was often told of the wealthy man who came to the Kuzmir Rebbe seeking punishment for his sins. Whereupon he replied: "You've already done harm to your soul; now you want to harm your body as well. Strive not to sin any more. But the Almighty does not want people to punish themselves. Give to charity and serve God dutifully—with joy."

There was no groaning or moaning to be heard at his court during the High Holy Day services. The prayers of penitence were not recited with lamentation, but in song. He composed new chants in honor of every Sabbath and Holy day and, if he ever failed to do so, which was seldom, he was a disturbed man that particular day.

The flow of Hasidim arriving at his court throughout some fifty years also brought about the revival of Janowiec on the opposite side of the Vistula, for the road to Kazimierz from Warsaw and other towns on its left bank led through Janowiec, whose marketplace was crowded all year round with wagons bringing thousands of Hasidim to Reb Ezekiel's court. They stayed overnight at Jewish inns, and were ferried across the river to Kazimierz the following morning.

Janowiec belonged to the enigmas of Jewish life in Poland. The settlement had grown up around the 16th century manor of Court Piotr Firlej, who had encouraged Jews to settle in the town by leasing his estates to them. During its most prosperous period, Janowiec never exceeded a thousand inhabitants, among whom there were less than a hundred Jewish families. And yet, there was an old stone synagogue there, even more splendid than the one in Kazimierz. The buttresses at its four corners and its two-level roof were marks of its 16th-century origin. The carved wooden ornaments over the Holy Ark, and colorful frescoes of birds, fish and animals interwoven with passages from the Scriptures, were preserved in the Janowiec synagogue until the Nazi invasion.

When Reb Ezekiel died in 1856 at the age of eighty-four, Kazimierz vanished temporarily from the hasidic scene. His eldest son, Reb Samuel Elijah, moved to Zwolin, and from there the Kuzmir dynasty was carried on in Modzic, where a new tradition of chanting was launched. Not until the 1880's did another hasidic Rebbe, the son of the Trisk *tzadik*, Reb Mottele Twerski of Tchernobil, settle in Kazimierz. By this time, however, the route from Warsaw to Kazimierz no longer led through Janowiec but through Pulawy, which was on the newly-constructed Warsaw-Lublin railroad.

In comparison with the humble wooden buildings of Reb Ezekiel's court, Reb Mottele's stone edifice seemed like a fortress. He had taken over the former town hall, whose offices had been transferred to the Przybylo houses on the marketplace following the 1863 Uprising, and continued to maintain his court in Kazimierz for nearly thirty years. During that time dozens of his loyal Hasidim settled there, among them merchants who took the Rebbe into their businesses as partner. They revived the town's dormant trade, and raised the living standard of the community.

This second period of hasidism in Kazimierz lasted until 1905, when the town became embroiled in strikes and rebellions against the czarist regime. Reb Mottele departed for Warsaw, but the people of Kazimierz continued to glorify the rabbinical court and even the wealth of the Rebbe, for he used to ride in a gilt carriage drawn by five horses just like the gentile squires.

8

JEWISH-POLISH IDYLL

By the end of the 19th century, Kazimierz was discovered by the leading Polish writers of the day: Boleslaw Prus, Henryk Sien kiewicz, and Alexander Swiętochowski. Such artists as Jozef Brandt and Wojciech Gerson began to paint its landscapes and its manors with their fantastic bas-reliefs. The growing popularity of the town among Polish intellectuals inspired the enterprising Berens, a Pole of Swedish descent, to build the town's first hotel and restaurant next to the Fara Church on the hill overlooking the marketplace. The veranda of this restaurant was the scene for discussions among writers of the Mloda Polska group (Young Poland), who gave a new impetus to the struggle for an independent Poland; Stanislaw Przybyszewski, Stefan Zeromski, Gustaw Danilowski, and other authors destined to become famous.

Although it was integral to Polish history, both in fact and legend, there is no mention of Jewish Kazimierz in the works of any of these writers; they ignored the phenomenon of the harmonious relationship between the Jews and gentiles of the town and its nearby villages.

Unlike other small centers, the Kazimierz community did not dread the three churches to the east, north, and south. Besides the steel crucifixes on the steeples, three huge oak crosses on the highest hill overlooking the town had been erected to commemorate the victims of the 1707 plague; only the west view of the marketplace stretched away unobstructed. During the week Jews grazed their goats on the Mountain of the Three Crosses. On Friday evenings its slopes were crowded with visitors savoring the picturesque town in the valley; the stores were closed in the deserted marketplace, and Sabbath candles flickered in the windows of houses that clustered under a domed blue sky, whose edge was ablaze in the setting sun on the opposite bank of the Vistula. The sound of church bells fused with the chanting in Jewish houses of prayer. The two disparate worlds coexisted in an atmosphere of peace. The town's Polish intelligentsia attended the majestic weddings in the historic synagogue, and came to hear *Kol Nidre* services on the eve of the Day of Atonement, and to see the procession with the Torah scrolls on *Simhat Torah*. Jewish boys and girls went to the church weddings of their Polish friends and even attended Christmas Eve masses.

When a Christian funeral procession wound through the marketplace, Jewish shops closed as a mark of sorrow; and when Jewish hearses passed by, Polish onlookers doffed their hats. The annual Corpus Christi festival did not evoke the slightest anxiety among the Jews of Kazimierz as it did in other towns, where such celebrations often ended in assaults upon them. Here young Jews surveyed the ceremonial from their balconies and rooftops—a familiar sight to them.

Thus a sense of mutual respect had developed gradually between the Polish and Jewish inhabitants. From time to time there was gossip about a love affair between a Jewish boy and Polish girl, or vice versa; but there were no mixed marriages in Kazimierz. For generations Jews lived closely with their Polish neighbors, contributing their share to the growth of the town's economy; Jewish horticulturists prevailed upon estate owners and peasants to convert their wheatfields into orchards; enterprising Jewish merchants brought plantings of new species of fruit from Hungary and in time Kazimierz became famous for its Hungarian plums, the so-called *wegierki* that were dried in primitive earthen ovens, stored with winter apples and pears, in the local stone granaries, and then transported to Warsaw by bark.

The Jews also altered the architectural face of their town, building wooden balconies onto the crumbling walls of the ruined mansions they bought, and winding staircases leading to rooms that were piled like nests, one atop the other. They set up their stores under the Gothic arches; Jewish joiners and Polish carpenters imitated the style prevalent in the marketplace by building houses with doubletiered roofs and projecting eaves supported by oak pillars.

Later, a distinctive Romantic style developed out of these improvised wooden additions to the thick walls. It blended harmoniously with the surrounding landscape. On the narrow side streets, wooden houses with shingled, moss-covered roofs merged into the deep valleys, lavishly covered with juicy grass, wild roses and berberry shrubs. The more affluent Jewish women made wonderful jam both from rose leaves and the flame-red berberries whose tiny, hard cores had to be pried out patiently with needles. Wild fruit trees—apple, pear, and nut—grew on the slopes and, around the base of their trunks, blackberries and wild strawberries. In the evenings, beetles made a monotonous buzz in the valleys, frequently interrupted by the hooting of owls and calls of other nightbirds. Breezes wafted the scents of jasmine, acacia and lilac into town, and on moonless nights the deep darkness was pierced by the glow of fireflies.

9

WHEN THE RIVER SPOKE YIDDISH

The river that whispered in Yiddish is Wisla (Vistula) the main water-artery of Poland, glorified by an anonymous bard as "The Queen of our Rivers", on whose banks Jews dwelt for centuries. She runs throughout the lands of Poland from the southern tip to the Baltic Sea in the North, gathering on her way the waters of hundreds of streams and tributaries. Her sources stem from the western mountain-ridge of Karpaty, the so-called Beskidy, near the village Wisla. In the early archaic Yiddish that sprouted in the first Jewish communities at the southernmost flow of the Vistula, they called the river: "Weisl".

The Jews who came to Poland in the Middle Ages, driven out of Germany, brought with them skills in various crafts and experience in trade, and early Polish rulers encouraged them to establish shops and develop industry. They were engaged in weaving, tailoring and baking, and made tools that had been previously imported from Germany; they were particularly effective in developing trade in grains, timber, salt, fruits and livestock, transported in barges, sailboats and rafts down the Vistula, as far as the port of Danzig on the Baltic Sea—a stretch of waterway that took 250 days to traverse.

Despite the restrictions imposed by Polish rulers under the pressure of the Church, dozens of Jewish communities sprang up on the lands that flanked the Vistula—the lifeline of the Polish Kingdom. With the passing of time the German language of the Jewish settlers absorbed Slavic words used in everyday life, interspersed with expressions drawn from Hebrew prayers. Out of this mixture a new language, a jargon, began to emerge, and developed in time into an original, colorful, idiomatic language, named "Yiddish," characterized by its folklore flavor and sharp sense of irony. It spread as early as the 16th century among Jews in other non-German-speaking lands, such as the Slavic countries in the East, Italy in the South and the Netherlands in the West.

This new Jewish language in the Diaspora was referred to for the first time as "Yiddish" in a Hebrew booklet published in 1649 in Amsterdam, where three decades later the first Yiddish daily paper in the world made its appearance. The booklet is a shattering eyewitness account of the survivors of the pogroms perpetrated by the Ukranian Cossacks under Bogdan Chmielnicki, in which hundreds of Jewish communities in Poland, Lithuania and the Ukraine were destroyed. The author of *The Lament* tells how the Cossacks, "jeered at the Jews, mocking their Yiddish."

It is a tragic fact that some three centuries later, at the pinnacle of the refinement of the Yiddish language and the blossoming of its literature, the creators of Yiddish culture and three Yiddish-speaking generations were destroyed by the Nazis on ground adjoining one of the oldest Jewish communities on the Vistula—Oświęcim (Auschwitz), a name now synonymous with the genocide of the Jewish people, the site of the largest death-factory in Nazi-occupied Europe.

Official Nazi documents attest to the fact that Auschwitz was designated primarily to consummate the program for the total annihilation of European Jewry. This special aspect of Auschwitz was virtually overlooked in the common postwar impression that this charnel house on the Vistula was just one more extermination camp, only more horrendous in its symbolism. And yet the primary importance of Auschwitz was confirmed by the Commandant of

The reconstructed Great Synagogue in Kazimierz was converted into a movie-house, named "Visla" (Visula).

the camp, Rudolf Hess (not to be confused with the Deputy-Führer), who was tried and hanged in Poland. While in jail in Cracow, awaiting execution,—and this in 1946—he wrote his memoirs in which he quoted a conversation with Adolf Hitler in the summer of 1941, when the Auschwitz death-factory was already in full operation: "The Fuhrer ordered the Final Solution of the Jewish Problem and we, the S.S., had to carry out this order. The extermination camps in the East could not accomplish this task, I have therefore chosen Auschwitz for that purpose, because of its advantageous position for transportation and particularly in view of the possibility of isolating and camouflaging the area."

Even today this truth is being camouflaged by party-line Polish historians and custodians of the Auschwitz Museum, who convey the impression that the Jews were only a paragraph in the genocide scenario planned against all the Polish people.

Auschwitz was a mammoth industrial complex, where four million slave-laborers of various nationalities, the majority of them Jews, went through the hell of starvation, debasement and exhaustion, to be finally destroyed in the gas-chambers and crematoria. The Auschwitz Moloch was erected on the marshes of the river Sola, a tributary of the Vistula where Jews settled as early as the 13th century. Truly, it may be said the Vistula was the river where the voice of Yiddish was first heard. Oswięcim was then the capital of a Slavic Duchy all of which bore the same name. The ruler over that land accorded homeless Jews the right to settle in his domain by an act of special *Privilege,* later honored by the Polish king, who purchased the duchy in 1457, and encouraged Jews to develop there the weekly fairs that attracted merchants from near and far.

Over a century later, in 1563, King Sigismund August II confirmed the *Privilege* for Jews to live in Oswięcim, but denied them the right to own houses in the market-square or to build a synagogue; he also barred the influx of Jewish settlers. The Jews fought vigorously against such restrictions, stressing their contribution to the development of the city from the time of its foundation. The restrictions were finally lifted and in 1588 the Jews were permitted to build a sumptuous synagogue and to acquire ground for a new cemetery; thus Oswięcim, became the spiritual center of the surrounding Jewish communities.

At the outbreak of World War II the Jewish population of Oswięcim amounted to almost half of the 12,000 residents. After the
Liberation it developed into an important industrial center with a
population of over 30,000—without a single Jew.

There are few native Jews of Oswięcim left; there is no memorial
book of the ancient community, although the survivors of hundreds
of smaller *shtetlekh* on the banks of the Vistula did memorialize
their home-towns, where the sounds of Yiddish reverberated for
centuries.

****

One of the most picturesque of these *shtetlekh*, rich in the best
aspects of Jewish-Polish ethnic intimacy, was Kazimierz. It had
attracted Jewish writers and artists and captured their imagination
with the romantic legends of "Esterka" and the King; the deep-
rooted hasidic traditions; the beauty of the colorful landscape that
marks the hilly right bank of the Vistula.

Sholem Asch was the first Yiddish writer to visit the town at the
beginning of the 20th century. He spent several summers there and
once brought with him I. L. Peretz, recognized as the father of
modern Yiddish literature. *At Night in the Old Marketplace*,
Peretz's mystical drama, evokes the ambiance of Jewish Kazimierz, which was a source of many of Sholem Asch's novels and
short stories. Its Jews served as prototypes for the characters he
developed, beginning with his early, masterful novelette, *A Shtetl*,
and ending with the novel, *Salvation* (the title in Yiddish is: *Der
T'hilim Yid*). Several episodes in his tempestuous life took place in
Kazimierz. His affair with the beautiful Stefania Feuerstein shook
the whole community; and elderly Jews recalled with anger his
heretical trick on a summery Friday evening when he put on a satin
gabardine and fur-edged cap and trotted around the synagogue on
horseback while people were entering it for Sabbath services. They
threw stones at him, shouting furiously: "Apostate! Apostate!".
After this incident the embarrassed Asch stopped coming to Kazimierz for a time. Several summers later he returned and, as indicated above, the life of the town was a significant influence upon his
subsequent literary work.

When his mentor, the noted Polish writer, Stanislaw Ignacy Wit-kiewicz, suggested that he write in Polish, Asch replied: "In Kazimierz the Vistula speaks to me in Yiddish". His *Shtetl* is the first story about Jewish life in a small Polish town and the first in the modern Yiddish literature to be translated into Russian and German immediately upon publication. It deals with a wealthy timber merchant, Ezekicl Gombiner, and its plot is enriched by an array of characters depicted in the turbulence of their daily life, their moods and dreams, and heightened by masterly descriptions of nature. Asch saw Kazimierz as the perfect embodiment of harmonious life in a *shtetl*, achieved through century-long strife and resistance. It had evolved into a distinctive organism with its own language, customs and dress, its own sources of physical and spiritual sustenance.

In his *Shtetl* Asch used episodes and characters from other towns as well. Kazimierz is mentioned here and there, incidentally, the topographical identity of the town blurred; the names of the protagonists are, of course, fictitious, except for one person: Chaim, the ferryman, whose family had for generations held a lease on the ferry traffic from one bank of the Vistula to the other. He had no equal in the towns along the river where the ferries were run by gentiles. His house was in the village of Wojszyn on the opposite bank, near Janowiec, the only house with a wooden roof among all the thatched village huts; Asch's description of him and his home is authentic throughout:

"A family has lived in this house for years. They live there with themselves and with the river as neighbor. Chaim, the ferryman's house, they call it today. Thirty years ago it was Moshe the ferryman's house. The names change as the years go by, but the house, the water, and the label 'Ferryman' remain the same. The present ferryman is called Chaim. He is a man of fifty, tall, lean, with a fluttery, broad, gray beard."

That is how he looked even on the eve of the Nazi invasion. Chaim was a man in his eighties then. He still wore the same round hat and long gaberdine, its hem tucked into his belt while he stood in the boat, slicing the waves with a long oar, his back slightly bent, his high forehead deeply creased, his cheeks sunken. By then he was no longer the only ferryman in town. The cross-river traffic was now partly in the hands of non-Jews.

At the end of his life, Chaim, who had inherited dozens of boats from his father, had one left. He still inhabited the same little house in Wojszyn. His wife, who had delivered several generations of children in the village, was now buried in the Janowiec cemetery. Sholem Asch describes the ferryman's Vistula idyll:

"The river behaves in a Jewish manner; like a Jew, according to Jewish tradition, it observes the Sabbath and the Holy Days. It flows gently . . . one wave kisses another. Chaim and his wife sit in front of their door. He reads the Bible, she the Yiddish version of the Pentateuch. They tell the river tales of God's wonders, and each wave seizes a word and pushes on."

Chaim the ferryman was the most popular figure among both Jewish and non-Jewish guests in Kazimierz. Artists painted his portrait, writers admired the vigor of his Polish, particularly his peasant dialect, replete with pithy, idiomatic expressions and clever folk-sayings.

Before Sholem Asch wrote his "Shtetl," another visitor, the Polish novelist Wladyslaw Reymont, had already published the first chapters of his great novel, *The Peasants.* For hours he sailed the Vistula with Chaim, jotting down the ferryman's earthy expressions. He was astonished by the peasant idioms and wit that flowed so naturally from the lips of this Jew of the Vistula.

His Yiddish was as rich in folk-sayings and figures of speech as his Polish. Years later Solomon Rosenberg, the translator of Reymont's Nobel Prize winning *Peasants* into Yiddish, came to Kazimierz to ask Chaim for the Yiddish equivalents of those juicy, often complex peasant expressions.

Reymont's and Sholem Asch's books represented the best in the then fashionable regionalism in Polish literature and art, of which the pioneer was Stanislaw Ignacy Witkiewicz, bard of Zakopane and portrayer of the mountaineers in the Tatra region, the first Polish writer to show an ardent interest in the rise of modern Yiddish literature. He detected its kinship with Polish regionalism and befriended the young Sholem Asch, who became a frequent visitor at his homes in Cracow and Zakopane; it was he who first brought Asch to Kazimierz. Witkiewicz's fascination with the

phenomenon of the Yiddish literature emerging on Polish soil and his deep sentiment for Sholem Asch in particular is expressed in a letter to Wilhelm Feldman, then the foremost literary critic and historian of modern Polish literature. The non-Jew Witkiewicz drew the attention of the assimilated Jew, Feldman, born in a hasidic family, to the importance of the work of the talented young Yiddish writers being ignored in Polish literary circles. In the letter, dated November 9, 1903 in Zakopane, Witkiewicz wrote: "I met a highly gifted Jewish writer, Sholem Asch. He read to me the first act of his play, written in *jargon*. My conversation with him and the content of the first act was for me a discovery of a new world. I know many Jewish types, formed under the pressure of the difficult conditions in which the Jewish people live. But Asch is for me something entirely new. I can say that for the first time I felt so close to the Jewish soul that revealed itself to me without the slightest hypocrisy, as it is: rather proud than ashamed of all the peculiarities they have developed during the millenia of ghetto existence."

Witkiewicz then attempts to win Feldman's support in presenting Asch's play on the Polish stage in Cracow:

"The first act is a complete entity in itself, that is worthwhile to be seen not only by the Jews who speak jargon, but by everybody, particularly in our society, where the Jews represent one of the most tragic problems that is not understood or taken seriously by our own Polish people, who seem to satisfy themselves either with a theoretical philo-Semitism, that has more and more become a rarity, or with a candid programmatic anti-Semitism."

After Asch's novel "A Shtetl" appeared, Kazimierz became a favorite resort for Jewish writers and artists, who portrayed its Jewish characters. One of the artists, Maurycy Minkowski, a deaf-mute, painted with poetic insight. His ears sealed against the melodramatic exaggerations of tourist guides, who each summer improvised ever more fantastic tales about the town, with rare intuition Minkowski captured *shtetl* life on his large canvases—the blessing of Sabbath candles, the lamentations on the Day of Atonement, the exchanging of gifts on Purim, the noisy Friday fish markets, boys and girls hurrying to bakeries with the Sabbath *cholent,* women in bonnets and Turkish shawls, the men in festive dress going to services, a multitude of local characters in the marketplace, merchants, coachmen, water carriers at the well, with its wooden roof embellished with stylized carvings—and surpassed all the other artists in penetrating to the core of Jewish Kazimierz.

10

THE BARD OF KAZIMIERZ

Destined to become one of the leading Yiddish writers, Zusman Segalovitch, came from smoky, industrial Bialystok at the beginning of the 20th century and his imagination was stirred by the idyllic *shtetl* on the Vistula. He spoke of local characters by their real names as well as nicknames, which were not always complimentary; and in the end immortalized Kazimierz in poetry and prose.

He made his debut in 1909 with a ballad based on an incident that had occurred in the town. The daughter of a pious Jew had drowned herself over an unhappy love affair. Although the poet changed the name of the ill-fated heroine to Reyzele, a note at the end, "written in Kazimierz," gave it the stamp of authenticity.

In another poem, entitled "Kazimierz," Segalovitch revealed himself fully by his portrayal of a small town: its historic ruins, its churches and synagogue, and an array of characters— shopkeepers, pious Jews and "enlightened" younger ones, dreamy girls, coachmen, and orchard laborers. Although Segalovitch felt at home in Kazimierz, his arrival was always an event in the town:

Now back in Kazimierz, wait driver, go easy,
Your horses are wildly racing downhill,
And so many children come running and greet me,
Shouting: "The Squire!" To them it's a thrill.
This "squire" owns a castle high in the sky,
My golden house swings over there in the west.
Here on earth I am poor like your fathers,
Though I may seem rich, and splendidly dressed.

"Kazimierz" struck a totally original epic note in Yiddish poetry; legend and fact intertwined.

You don't know the town then? That's really a pity.
A myriad of tales live here and breathe.
Vast mountains and orchards reflect in the river,
A roofless palace extends to the sky.
In this palace there once lived the noblest of kings,
Now crows have cawed there for the longest time . . .
And sometimes at night a star falls into the ruins,
But no one finds this celestial treasure.
True Jewish piety lives on here still
And dies like an ancient oak by the road,
Here you can still see a lonesome, scared deer,
That flees man's gaze with mounting fright.

The lonely synagogue seemed abandoned among the mighty stone churches and evoked sad feelings in the visitor from the big city. Awed by the splendid nature of the region, the poet had problems, however, in identifying the flowers and birds in the Yiddish language:

Three churches of Kazimierz, and all three
Ringed by trees, by many trees backed;
And our house of prayer—alas—stands alone,
Shunted off to a corner, its roof cracked, decaying . . .
A slow-moving tune dies in the frames
Of windows thrown open . . . I walk swiftly by,
This mournful tune does not follow me far,
It quickly melts into the singing of May.
What are the birds called? And the names of flowers?
Our language offers no labels for these.
I'm destined to rejoice, just like a mute,
And like a mute to conceal my pain.

From then on, Segalovitch's poems, stories and novels were filled with descriptions of Kazimierz, which became the source of his

inspiration, the background for most of his writings, and his Yiddish became spicier because he adopted expressions from the language as it was spoken in Poland. He depicted the first symptoms of Jewish middle-class assimilation to Polish life—the scrambling for acceptance in the pervasive culture—which he observed in youngsters from Warsaw and other big cities, who came to Kazimierz for their summer vacations. For him the *shtetl* was a prism through which he saw Jewish Poland; and when he wandered through Lithuania and Russia during the holocaust years, managing later to reach the land of Israel, Kazimierz was the focus for his burning visions, the moving force for his Job-like laments. From his exile he sent greetings to his Jewish and non-Jewish heroes in Kazimierz, and out of his intense nostalgia now called them by their right names:

> *Deborah in her shop growing gently older,*
> *Sukher who brings young calves in to market,*
> *Vovtche the coachman, my most loyal fan,*
> *Janek the drunkard and street-cleaner man.*
> *Nahum the master of the boats by the water,*
> *Abraham-Avreml who puts rhymes in order.*
> *Andzia for whom Warsaw is but a stroll—*
> *My very warm greetings to all of you, all . . .*

A Tree in Poland, his powerful poem on the holocaust, invokes the *shtetl* in its opening lines:

> *In Kazimierz, on the road to Czerniawy,*
> *A tall birch stands a-greening . . .*

For Segalovitch this was a return to his early poem *Kazimierz*, which had expressed his feelings for the town.

11

YEARS OF TURMOIL

Off the beaten track, on the bank of the Vistula, far from the watchful eye of the Czarist secret police, rural Kazimierz became a gathering place for Polish as well as Jewish revolutionaries. Two students who happened to meet there one summer later played a leading role in the struggles against the Czarist regime, within the Jewish labor movement in particular; one was Henryk Ehrlich, the son of an orthodox family in Lublin. The other, Bronislaw Grosser, was the son of an assimilated middle-class family in Warsaw.

Ehrlich had just graduated from the Polish *Gymnasium*, and had come to Kazimierz to rest before taking his university entrance examinations. Grosser was spending his vacation with a group of young Polish revolutionaries, and his future was in great part determined by his chance meeting with the older Ehrlich who convinced him to draw closer to the Jewish milieu. The two students joined the social democratic *Bund*, and soon distinguished themselves as its leading theoreticians. During World War II, Ehrlich sought refuge from the Nazis in the Soviet Union. Ironically he became one of Stalin's first Jewish victims.

Kazimierz was also the site for the first revolutionary activities of Felix Dzierzynski, who became the founder and much feared chief of the Soviet Security Police, the *Cheka*. One of the heads of the Polish Social Democratic Party (S.D.K.P.L.), he organized strikes in the tanneries, breweries, and sugar factories of Kazimierz and nearby estates, and also set up revolutionary cells among students and professors at the Agricultural Institute, located on the former estate of Prince Adam Czartoryski in nearby Pulawy. These activities led to a planned rebellion, in which Dzierzynski managed to enlist officers from the garrison of the czarist army in Pulawy, students from the Agricultural Institute there, and peasants from neighboring villages. Foremost among the army officers was Antonov-Ovseenko, who was to become one of the heroes of the October 1917 Revolution. He was Lenin's military adviser and led the successful assault upon the Winter Palace in St. Petersburg. During the Spanish Civil War of 1936-1939, he was the U.S.S.R.'s Consul General in Barcelona. When we met there, the veteran Bolshevik spoke with unusual warmth about Kazimierz, where he used to have his conspiratorial meetings with Felix Dzierzynski. In 1937, Ovseenko was suddenly recalled to Moscow and promptly liquidated.

In 1905, back in Kazimierz, a group of young men planned an insurrection against the government, but the plot was uncovered, and many arrests were made. Several Jews were sent to Siberia, and the rest escaped to America.

The gathering tempest of revolutionary events lured some Russian Jewish intellectuals to Kazimierz. Their arrival was like a fresh breeze in the stagnating atmosphere of the *shtetl*. Three in particular introduced a new element into the community's life: Stanislaw Lichtson, the first Jewish pharmacist in town; the agronomist Levenstein, a former manager of the noted Brodsky breweries in Kiev; and Chaim Szenderowicz, who owned the first Jewish guest house in Kazimierz. He was to exert a profound spiritual influence upon the younger generation of Kazimierz Jewry. Lichtson's pharmacy was located in Bromberg's Danzig House. A huge, hissing kerosene lamp hung from the high, vaulted ceiling—the only one of its kind in town—at night it cast long streaks of light across the marketplace. Next door lived the barber-surgeon, Moshke

Barszcz, known far and wide as a healer. All the area's gentry and rabbis from neighboring towns counted themselves among his patients.

Levenstein settled in the surrounding mountains and set up an experimental nursery with hothouses, raising exotic plants and flowers, and cross-fertilizing various fruits. He worked in collaboration with the Agricultural Institute in Pulawy, and received visits from the professors who, people said, were disguised revolutionaries hatching seditious plots against the Czar.

A visit to the Levensteins was a rare treat for the town's young Jews. The tall master of the house, who spoke Polish with a Russian accent, was a warm, indulgent man, engaging in conversations with the youngsters who visited his gardens during their Sabbath hikes. Mrs. Levenstein, a small woman with gray hair braided on top of her head, seemed at first glance forbidding, even unfriendly. She made the boys take off their caps the moment they stepped onto her veranda, and lectured them about the religious fanaticism of their parents; yet she treated her guests to rare fruits never seen in Kazimierz: peaches and strawberries. She also lent them books from her large library—Polish classics such as the works of Kraszewski, Adam Mickiewicz and Henryk Sienkiewicz—mentioning with pride that Sienkiewicz, the first Polish Nobel Prize winner for Literature, had been to their house.

The chief attraction of the Levensteins' villa was the magnificent peacocks that were kept in a huge wire cage. There was an old-fashioned well nearby with a wooden wheel; against the background of multi-colored flowers and fruit trees it was a living illustration of the poem "I have a Garden with a Well," by the great Hebrew poet, Chaim Nachman Bialik.

Lichtson and Levenstein set themselves apart from the town's Jews. They socialized with the priest, the doctor, the local teachers and gentry. They came to the synagogue only on the Day of Atonement, wearing slim prayer shawls of a kind never seen in Kazimierz. As to Szenderowicz, he flaunted his heretical conduct. Immediately upon his arrival in town he gathered Jewish youths around him, and introduced them to the political Zionism of Theodor Herzl. The Szenderowicz family later revolutionized the established Jewish lifestyle of Kazimierz. Chaim Szenderowicz's children, who had been educated in Warsaw and Prague, established the first modern Jewish school that used Polish as its language of instruction and offered an extensive curriculum of Hebrew and Jewish history. The eldest daughter, Sonia, and her young brother Zygmunt, were the catalysts in this educational venture. Before his early death, Zygmunt also established a branch of the *Hashomer Hatza'ir* in Kazimierz, one of the first branches of the newly-founded radical Zionist youth movement. The youngest of the Szenderowiczs, Pola, was the first *halutz,* or pioneer, from the town to settle in Palestine, where she helped found the well-known *Kibbutz Mishmar Haemek.*

At first, the pious Kazimierz Jews resented the mounting influence of the Szenderowicz family over their young; Chaim Szenderowicz had vehement disputes with the local zealots in the marketplace, and the youth greatly enjoyed listening to them, especially proud of the fact that the clean-shaven rebel outargued pious, bearded scholars with his knowledge of the Scriptures.

Originally, the Szenderowiczs lived in Warsaw all year round and came to Kazimierz only to operate their summer guest house on a hilltop in the Czerniawy range. Its spring of delicious fresh water was ice cold, even on the hottest day. For the young Jews the hotel opened the way to secular Jewishness and Polish culture. Prominent personalities from Warsaw spent their vacations there—writers, artists, and professionals, among them both Zionist leaders and assimilationists. Several evenings a week Chaim Szenderowicz, who had published some Hebrew poems under a pen name, gave free Hebrew lessons to local boys and girls. He was said to be a close friend of I. L. Peretz, and he did, in fact, imitate the writer, growing a mustache, wearing his hair long, and sporting a long, black cape. Besides the Hebrew lessons he also taught various secular subjects to students who came to stay at his hotel.

The outbreak of World War I tore apart the half-spun web of secular Jewish life in our *shtetl.* My earliest memories are of German and Austrian bombardments of Russian-ruled Kazimierz. We hid in the cellar; czarist regiments marched by day and night; stores were hurriedly closed up whenever hooves were heard on the cobblestones of the Pulawy Road and the dreaded word, "Cossacks," passed from mouth to mouth.

A 19th Century engraving of Kazimierz showing the ruins of the royal palace (center, rear), the tower (left, rear), and the Fara Church (right).

In those stricken hours, a rumor spread that Nikolai Nikolayevitch, the Czar's uncle and commander-in-chief of the Russian armies, was riding across the market square astride his white charger at the head of a Cossack regiment. His alleged presence saved the town from certain pogrom. Whether this actually happened has never been confirmed; however, the story fits well into the pattern of Kazimierz's history, in which fact and fiction have always been mingled.

As the front drew closer, the Jews were evacuated—but they came back as soon as the Austrians had occupied the region. It was at that time in Kazimierz that the Esther legend came to pass in a new and true version: the local Austrian commandant fell in love with the beautiful daughter of a kosher butcher. The Austrian occupation forces relaxed their rigid rule, trade picked up briskly, and the Jews began to rebuild their demolished houses.

In 1916, the *shtetl* was shaken by a catastrophe. Suddenly one autumn evening, the bells of all three local churches began to peal as they did whenever there was a fire. The terrifying news spread fast: one of Chaim the ferryman's disastrously overloaded barks had capsized. The passengers aboard were Jews returning from work on the construction of military fortifications on the other side of the Vistula, near Janowiec. Nearly every family in town had one or two members on that boat. The whole community, every last man, woman and child, ran down to the river with kerosene lanterns. Desperate cries from the shore mingled with the echoing shouts of fishermen on both banks helping to rescue the survivors. By midnight, more than half of the two hundred victims had been dragged out of the water. Lamenting Jews raced back and forth among the corpses laid out near Elbaum's brewery, identifying their dear ones. All that week there were funerals. The disaster was inscribed on the last page of the parchment prayerbook in the synagogue, which contained the chronicles of the community.

At that time, events of historic significance were taking place in the outside world: the Russian Revolution, February 1917; the British Balfour Declaration, November 1917, with the promise of a Jewish homeland in Palestine; and the rebirth of an independent Poland at the close of World War I. These three turning points in modern European history are superimposed upon each other on the screen of my memory as if they had taken place at the same instant.

Of all the striking events of the time, the *Hanukah* festivities in Kazimierz during the winter of 1917 have left an indelible imprint on my mind. We were celebrating the Balfour Declaration. The messianic age seemed close at hand as Chaim Szenderowicz stood on the *almemar* in his broad-brimmed fedora and wide poet's bow next to the fragile, gray-haired Rabbi Chaim Leyb Zilbermintz in his traditional, heavy, fur-edged hat.

His voice trembling, the Rabbi made the benediction, lit the first *Hanukah* candle, then spoke in a whisper for a long time. By contrast, Szenderowicz's voice boomed as he launched into his speech, first in Hebrew, then in Yiddish. He said the dream of the return to Zion was about to be realized; it was the duty of every Jew to contribute generously toward this effort. Gold brooches, chains and diamond rings were promptly dropped from the women's gallery, and the men surrendered their gold and silver watches. The large bowls, used on the eve of the Day of Atonement for charitable collections, were quickly filled.

Another event of that time has remained vivid in my memory, namely the visit of a Jewish officer from the Lublin headquarters of the Austrian occupation forces. One Saturday morning in the late summer of 1918 a stocky officer with a trimmed beard came to the services in the synagogue. He wore a prayer-shawl over his uniform with golden epaulets and medals on his breast. The people whispered about him: he was a captain, considered an unusually high rank for a Jew. He was given a place of honor at the eastern wall of the synagogue, next to the elders of the community, and addressed the worshippers in Yiddish. My father, who was the reader of the *Torah* on holidays and festive occasions, repeated with excitement the remarks of the officer about the glorious past of the Jewish community of Kazimierz, stressing Esterka's devotion to her people. The talk of the town was his prediction about the near fulfillment of the long cherished dream of a Jewish national home in Eretz Israel, symbolically coinciding with the imminent rebirth of an independent Poland.

Only years later did I learn the identity of this illustrious visitor. He was the renowned historian, Dr. Meyer Balaban, who served at that time as field-chaplain and special adviser on Jewish affairs for the Austrian Military Command of the Lublin region. During his service in Lublin Balaban had uncovered a wealth of source-material about the history of the ancient Jewish community there, particularly in the Renaissance period, for his work *The Jewish City of Lublin* that was published years later. This monograph with its detailed description of old synagogues, and tombstones at the graves of rabbinical scholars, doctors and astronomers, is now the most important monument for the Jewish community of Lublin, of which hardly any trace remains.

At my last meeting with Professor Balaban in Warsaw, in the winter of 1937, he recalled his visit to Kazimierz as an Austrian officer. Fascinated by its history and legend Balaban planned to write a monograph on Kazimierz, similar to his studies about other Jewish communities in Poland that earned him the reputation of the foremost historian of Polish Jewry. Shortly after his visit the town experienced the tremors of Polish independence. On the 7th of November, 1918, in nearby Lublin the first government of independent Poland was established and the Austrian army of occupation hastily withdrew. The Jews of Kazimierz reacted to Poland's independence with a mixture of joy and dread. They considered themselves equal citizens of the new republic. Yet they became apprehensive when the first wave of patriotic enthusiasm gave way to moblike behavior. Local Poles who had disarmed the Austrian gendarmes paraded haughtily about the marketplace with their captured guns; the Jews felt that *they* were henceforth the unchallenged masters of the town.

12

SHATTERED ILLUSIONS

For about seven hundred years the Jews of Kazimierz had lived side by side with their Christian neighbors who, between the Middle Ages and modern times, displayed the full gamut of friendliness and hostility towards the Jews. Each time a Polish king extended the rights of the middle classes, the local population discriminated against Jewish artisans and merchants. Only during Poland's subjugation by the Russian czars did the liberal Polish intelligentsia—particularly the political emigres in France—speak of the common destiny of Jews and Poles, and call for brotherhood and a united struggle to achieve a free Poland. No sooner had the dream of independence been realized in 1918, when abuse of the newly-won liberty was resumed at the expense of the Jews. The Polish neighbor, who had only yesterday been meek and humble, suddenly turned into an angry town councilman or arrogant policeman. The Jewish storekeeper or worker quickly sensed that he was being degraded to the rank of second-class citizen; in addition to this humiliation, he had to bear the heaviest burden of taxation.

In towns that had barely dug themselves out of the ruins after

World War I, Jews suddenly found that they were facing stiff competition from a new class of Polish merchants, who set up their stands in the marketplaces or opened stores in town. A boycott slogan, *Swoj do Swego* (Stick to your Own), was disseminated by the anti-Semitic National Democratic Movement, known as *Endecja,* whose tactics were encouraged by the new Polish regime.

The Jews of Kazimierz suffered far less from this chauvinism, since at that time the entire population of the town made its living almost exclusively from summer guests and tourists, the majority of whom were Jewish. Many Poles in Kazimierz even spoke Yiddish fluently—a sign of peaceful co-existence with their Jewish neighbors.

And yet the illusion of unity between Poles and Jews began to erode at the very outset of Polish independence. An unusual incident in the summer of 1918 made this clear. Early one Saturday morning, a car with several Polish civilians pulled into the marketplace. Its occupants asked for Vovtche Bromberg. The news of the strangers' arrival spread swiftly through town, and a large crowd gathered in front of his home. The mysterious agents put him in their car and drove off. Christians were as upset as Jews. A joint committee was set up and immediately sent to the district seat in Pulawy to intervene with the authorities. A few days later, Vovtche Bromberg was freed and absolved of the charge; but the incident revealed the primitive nature of the new bureaucracy. The grotesque accusation might have served as a theme for a Gogol story: a telegram had been sent to Bromberg from Danzig; the name had aroused suspicion in the Pulawy telegraph office, where it was interpreted as a "Jewish plot" against the newly-named city of Bydgoszcz, in Pomerania, called Bromberg under German rule; the officials had alerted the proper authorities, who had reacted with dispatch.

Similar episodes involving false slurs upon Jews were not unusual in the reborn nation, particularly during the Russo-Polish War of 1920-21. More than once they ended in tragedy. And yet, despite the worsening economic condition of the Jewish population, Polish independence brought about an upswing in Jewish cultural and political activity that penetrated to the smallest and most remote *shtetlekh.* In marketplaces as well as houses of worship young people carried on heated debates; some of them became leaders of groups that formed the nucleus of Poland's secular Jewish culture. Libraries, day schools, and evening courses were started in wretched quarters rented with pennies saved from food budgets; single copies of Yiddish newspapers and magazines, bought by the less poor, were passed from hand to hand; they discussed every article, and searched for hidden meanings within each story, each poem. They founded theatrical workshops, choirs, and sport clubs. Since they could rarely afford the luxury of inviting a guest speaker from Warsaw, a visit by a lecturer from the nearest city was an event.

Kazimierz found itself in an especially enviable position because of the famous writers, actors, painters, and political celebrities who came to spend the summer there. Each year they transformed the town by improvising festivals, concerts, lectures, theatrical performances, and even art exhibitions, all attracting young people from neighboring communities.

One summer proved unforgettable: the new Yiddish repertory company, the *Vilner Truppe* (Vilna Repertory Theatre), directed by David Herman, gave a performance of Ansky's *The Dybbuk*. The actors stayed at Szenderowicz's guest house and rehearsed on his spacious veranda. The town's young hid underneath it to watch. People said that Noah Nachbush must have modeled his interpretation of Ansky's mystical messenger upon the town recluse, Aaron, the rabbi's son.

The older inhabitants of Kazimierz also felt at ease with the summer "Bohemians"; they posed for the painters, and recognized themselves without resentment in the articles and stories of Yiddish writers. But once there was almost a scandal: Z. Segalovitch realistically described a romantic incident involving Vevtchele the Coachman, or *Pijak* the Drunk, as he was called. Angrily he threatened to break Segalovitch's neck next time the writer came to Kazimierz. At their next meeting, however, Vevtchele had cooled off. He laughed heartily when Segalovitch playfully offered him a high fee for writing about *him*.

13

THE ESTHER LEGEND

Their contact with artists and writers stimulated the imagination of the tourist guides in Kazimierz. Each year they enlarged their treasure store of anecdotes about the history of this old Polish settlement of which the central motif in their improvisations was the Esther legend. The men who really excelled at this were the two Yankls—Yankl Schwartzman and Yankl Goldfarb—nicknamed the Middleman and the Japanese, respectively. "Middleman" alluded to Yankl Schwartzman's occupation as broker, while "Japanese" referred to the Russo-Japanese War of 1905, when Yankl Goldfarb had ardently supported Japan in local debates. The two professional guides spoke superb Polish spiced with idioms that impressed not only tourists but the Polish writers who came there on holiday.

The formulas of the guides' stories differed. The elder Yankl, who was of medium height and wore a neat, gray beard and pince-nez dangling from a black cord, solemnly described King Kazimierz's nightly visits to Esther's castle in Bochotnica, on a mountain overlooking the Vistula. As if his tale were historical fact,

Yankl earnestly assured his listeners that the "goodhearted king of the peasants" commissioned his Jewish goldsmith from Spain to spin the gold threads which Esther used to embroider the curtain of the Holy Ark in the synagogue of Kazimierz. The younger Yankl, on the other hand, was tall and had a dense, curly black beard and merry, wise eyes. He was by nature a wag, coloring his stories with descriptions of the kosher Jewish dishes, the Sabbath meal and "gefillte fish" that Esther prepared for King Kazimierz . . .

These additions to the Esther saga came to life in Kazimierz under Communist rule when a cooperative restaurant named Estherka was set up in the vaulted shop that had once belonged to wealthy Shie Friedman. The menu listed two specialties: *Ryba po zydowsku*—gefillte fish—and *cholent*—the traditional Sabbath dish made with meat, potatoes, and beans.

The Esther legend was perpetuated not only by the guides but by the tailor Leyb Getzeles, a short, thin man with a long beard—a personification of the wee, bearded figure found on half of the split peanut, known to Jews as the "Holy Land nut." Every Purim until his death, Leyb Getzeles directed a performance of *Queen Esther of Kazimierz*, a play that he improvised. Among my liveliest childhood recollections is this Purim play in which tiny Getzeles, taking the leading role of the King, suddenly emerged as a giant in his built-up boots; and Esther, played by a boy, showed her lord and master the golden Holy Ark curtain that she had made. This performance, staged in Vovtche Bromberg's huge living room, was attended by all who could crowd in. On this occasion the curtain was always taken out of the huge wooden trunk where it had lain all year.

The Esther legend was the topic of one of the earliest popular Yiddish novelists, Shomer. His novel *"The Jewish Queen"* was published in Warsaw in 1884. Shomer designates his work "a true narrative based on historical fact." Following the pattern of a novel based on historical events, his tale begins with an actual date: "The year was 1343, the month Nissan. It was Passover eve . . ." In accord with the widely disseminated legend, he speaks of Esther's father, Raphael, as a poor tailor burdened with six children, and describes his firstborn, twenty-year-old Esther, as "slim and gentle, with cheeks like blushing roses."

Shomer depicts the parents' first visit to their daughter in the palace and evokes the Biblical scene of Joseph's encounter with his brothers in Pharaoh's Egypt: "Yes, it is I, your daughter Esther . . . I want to say as Joseph once did: 'I am Joseph your brother, whom ye sold into Egypt . . . God did send me before you to preserve life.' " (Gen. 45:4,7).

Modern Jewish historians offer the popular version of Esther of Opoczno, the Jewish mistress of King Kazimierz the Great, who built a castle for her in Bochotnica close to his summer residence in Kazimierz. She bore the King two sons, Niemir and Pelka, who were raised as Christians; and two daughters, whom their mother with the consent of the King brought up in the Jewish faith.

It is to be assumed that for Jewish historians the prime source for the role of Esther, or Esterka, in the life of Kazimierz the Great, married to the German princess Adelaida of Hesse, was the foremost Polish chronicler of the early 15th century, Jan Dlugosz. For a time he was canon of Sandomierz on the Vistula, where Jews lived as early as the 11th century; he later became canon of Cracow, and finally Archbishop of Gniezno, the cradle of Polish Christianity. The unfriendly Dlugosz version of the Kazimierz-Esther love affair stemmed from the king's quarrels with the clergy who attempted in vain to influence him. This chronicle dwells at length on the king's favors to the Jews under the influence of Esther, who charmed him with her unusual beauty and bore him two sons and two daughters. Dlugosz, who wrote his chronicles almost a century after the death of king Kazimierz, was relatively restrained in his criticism in comparison with the anti-Semitic venom in the tales of the 16th and 17th centuries, fabricated by Catholic clerics and writers of primitive fiction in that period.

A great change in the treatment of the Esterka tale by Polish writers occurred in the 19th century, after the two abortive Polish uprisings against Czarist rule. The most prolific Polish author of historical novels, Jozef Ignacy Kraszewski, in his huge saga *The King of the Peasants* (1881), continuously being reissued in Communist Poland, depicts the king and his Jewish mistress with sympathy and even admiration. His influence can be detected in the first dramatic work about Kazimierz and Esther in Polish litera-

ture, namely *Esterka* by Stanislaw Kozlowski which appeared in
1886 but was never staged.

At the same period the eminent Polish historian Count Edward
Raczynski authenticated the Esther-Kazimierz relationship by a
meticulously researched genealogy of generations of prominent
Polish families stemming from Niemir and Pelka, the sons of King
Kazimierz and Esther. According to Raczynski, Niemir and Ab-
raham, the son of Abraham who was the son of Niemir's brother,
Pelka, were the owners of the castle and large land-holdings of
Zbąszyn province in Western Poland. Their heirs adopted the
family name of Zbąski from Zbąszyn, but curiously the first name
Abraham, was repeated in the family for generations, in which
there was much intermarriage as well as marriage into the leading
families of Polish nobility, who shared the land in the area.

A touch of tragic symbolism was added to the history of Zbąszyn
on the eve of World War II, when on the night of October 7, 1938,
over 12,000 Polish Jews who had lived for years in Germany but
kept their Polish citizenship, were forcibly taken out of their homes
by the Nazis and dumped on no-man's-land, between the German
border town of Neu-Bentschen and the town of Zbąszyn. The
anti-Semitic Polish regime refused to recognize the validity of their
Polish passports and the mass of homeless Jews were interned in
the dilapidated former army barracks of Zbąszyn. Jews from all
over Poland rushed help to the destitute refugees and the Poles in
Zbąszyn too showed deep sympathy. Food and other necessities
for the improvised Jewish community were provided by the owners
of the surrounding estates, the heirs of the Zbąskis, whose ancestors were the son and grandson of Esther and King Kazimierz. It
was the Zbąszyn Jews who were the first to be trapped by the
German invaders of Poland.

A curious sidelight on the terrible events emerged in late years
when the grandson of the historian who had set straight the record
of Esther and King Kazimierz—and bearing the same name, Count
Edward Raczynski—became the Foreign Minister, later the last
President, of the Polish government-in-exile in London.

Such is the strange tale of Estherka in the sad history of Jews in
Poland, where the two nations whose sufferings were so intimately
interwoven, could not find a common fraternity.

The Esther theme found sympathetic expression in the Polish dramatic poem, *Zydzi* (The Jews) by K. Glinski, published in 1901. Glinski's message is the tolerance displayed by Kazimierz toward the Jews. The king publicly condemns as false any charges that Jews are responsible for the plagues and the author has Esther say:

> *The King has given me his heart,*
> *And with it a thousand favors for Israel.*

The Esther legend also fired the imagination of two contemporary Yiddish poets, S. I. Imber and Aaron Zeitlin. Imber's poem, *Esther*, published in Brunn in 1918, is a ballad which reflects the influence of Poland's 19th century poet, Juliusz Slowacki. Here Esther's father is a blacksmith rather than a tailor. The poem accentuates the tragic events, deviating from the allegedly sweet, idyllic course of the royal love affair. Esther's mother drowns herself because she has lost her daughter, and King Kazimierz is killed while hunting—on the very spot where he first met Esther and, enchanted by her beauty, took her to his palace.

Aaron Zeitlin's *Esther and Kazimierz the Great*, published in Warsaw in 1932, is the only play on the subject in Yiddish literature. It exemplifies the traditional practice of blaming Jews for plagues caused by poisoned wells, and the drama presents this historic accusation.

The American Yiddish poet, Jacob Glatstein, stripped the Esther legend of its romantic trappings in his book *When Yash Came*, depicting the twilight reality of the town of Kazimierz with a blend of surrealistic imagery and folklore. He listened to the exaggerations of the Jewish tourist guides, but portrayed the benevolent king in his own way:

> King Kazimierz wore a paper Purim crown, and had a beard of silk. He was slightly fatuous and resembled King Ahaseurus. But he was passionately in love, and bore the Jewish maiden up, up, ever higher, where the castles in the air had just been completed . . . And, during those long days when the king carried out his royal designs in distant parts, Esther looked yearningly down at the well, at the weathered, little houses, and at her fellow-Jews. At night, she unbraided her hair and sang: "I go out onto the balcony to gaze at the shtetl." It was during such dismal periods of waiting, that she attached a letter to the tail of the golden peacock. It was addressed to the Jewish people for whom her heart yearned. But the king's sorcerer unfurled a violent storm over the

entire land. The peacock could not find its way, and the letter tore loose and was lost.

This grotesque, yet lyrical description expressed Glatstein's feelings about Poland when he first returned to Lublin, his birthplace, and the surrounding Jewish *shtetlekh*, on the eve of the Nazi invasion. In Kazimierz the great Yiddish poet sensed the shadow of death hovering over Polish Jewry:

> What actually happened in Kazimierz? Listen, and you'll understand. The Jew had his sordid little existence, while the Gentile led a life without anxiety. We never got any further than the town's limits. Beyond them lay death: a huge cemetery with our grandfathers and mothers. Take a stroll up to the town limits and come back. Don't you know that smell—the smell of the grave's foliage?

★ ★ ★ ★ ★

The mini-stage of Kazimierz saw the entire range of Jewish communal activities in Poland. With the town's economic decline in the period between the two World Wars, the impoverishment of once wealthy residents became apparent. The manager of the cooperative bank, Saul Friedman, himself the son of a man who had been well-to-do, consistently urged the main office in Warsaw to permit him to make more and larger loans. When the restrictions remained severe, he issued loans on his own authority. His work at the bank gave him insight into the day-to-day problems of local Jewry, and he depicted them in a long novel, *The People of Godlbozhitz*, published under his pen name Leyb Raskin.

It was the last Yiddish novel to appear in Poland when World War II broke out. Its characters are authentic and recognizable, although their names are disguised in this most remarkable novel which reflected the struggles, fears, and hopelessness that pervaded the daily life of the Jews in the *shtetlekh* doomed to extinction. Soon afterwards, the 33-year-old author perished at the hand of the Nazi invaders.

14

TWO MOONS—TWO WORLDS

In the final years before the Holocaust, the town marketplace
became a meeting ground for Yiddish writers and Polish authors of
Jewish descent. Although the latter occupied an ever-growing position in Polish letters, they felt the squeeze of anti-Semitism even
more than their Yiddish-writing colleagues. This brought the two
groups together in closely-knit Kazimierz as nowhere else in Poland, for in the big cities such as Warsaw, Cracow and Lodz they
were alienated from one another, living in separate cultural worlds.
But in Kazimierz on the terrace of Berens's restaurant, or under
the quaint wooden roofs of the two wells in the marketplace, you
could meet Moshe Broderson and Julian Tuwim telling each other
anecdotes, or Z. Segalovitch discussing assimilation with Antoni
Slonimski. The avant-garde poets, Anatol Stern and Adam Wazyk,
also sought inspiration in Kazimierz. Adolf Rudnicki was regarded
as practically a resident of the town. He was a descendant of an old
hasidic family in Galicia, and though he had avoided any identifica-
tion with Jews in his early stories and novels, when he came to

Kazimierz, he often attended services at the hasidic houses of prayer.

The novelist, Maria Kuncewicz, who owned a summer house in the town, portrayed her Jewish protagonists with a great deal of warmth. In the early 1930's, she published a book of short stories about Kazimierz, entitled *Two Moons*, which appeared in several editions and was reprinted in Communist Poland in 1960. By then there were no Jews left in the town.

In strong, lyrical prose marked by grotesque undertones, she described both the Jewish and Polish inhabitants, and in depicting the schism that separated the two faiths with the sincerity of a practicing Catholic, she stressed that, in the face of death, there was a spirit of brotherhood between Jews and Christians, and pointed out that they attended each other's funerals.

The gulf between the two faiths is revealed in a story about the prayers held in the Kazimierz synagogue on the Day of Atonement, and the services in the church nearby, the lamentations of the Jews and the whispered worshipping of the Christians. Maria Kuncewicz characterizes the contents of the Jewish prayers as an eternal plaint to God: "Send the Messiah down to us! Let him show us the way . . . how to transcend death, and how to continue with body and soul." In the church, however, there were no pleas to God to send down the Redeemer, for this "had already happened." In her introduction to the postwar edition of the book, she speaks with nostalgia about the vanished Jews of Kazimierz: "I turn back to the valley of the Vistula . . . to the ruins haunted by the enamored king and by Esther who seeks the bones of Chaim the ferryman, Moshe the watercarrier, and Sholom the candelabra dealer . . . I turn back to the marketplace; there on the restaurant balcony, lit up by the moon, the artists proceed with their eternal dialogue about rebuilding the world with more humanity."

That the alienation between Jews and Poles in the literary world was greatly diminished in Kazimierz was largely due to the influence of the director of the Warsaw Art Academy, Professor Tadeusz Pruszkowski, an avowed liberal who was executed in 1942 by the Nazis for his activities in the resistance movement. He built a white stone villa in Kazimierz, called the White House, as well as an airport for his private plane—the only such craft seen flying over

On the Vistula, a painting by Moshe Appelbaum.

the *shtetl* before the outbreak of war. An artist with a broad out-
look, Pruszkowski directed his students' attention to the Jewish
way of life, pointing out the old houses of the town and their
characteristic "Jewish" architecture, which he himself painted
with enthusiasm. I saw his Kazimierz canvases with their Jewish
motifs on the walls of his Warsaw home alongside a large Biblical
painting by the 17th century French master, Poussin, which showed
Moses smiting the stone to draw forth water. ("And Moses lifted up
his hand, and smote the rock with his rod twice," Numbers 20:11).
In his Kazimierz villa, there was a large collection of Jewish ritual
objects which he often included in his still-lifes.

It is ironic, therefore, that his Jewish students were the initiators
of the group known as the "Brotherhood of Saint Luke," which
strove to revolutionize the hackneyed contemporary church art.
Their leader, Jan Gotard, a frail man of medium height, had the pale
complexion of a yeshiva student, but wore the typical gentile cap
with its black, gleaming visor. His predominant themes were the
old Kazimierz churches, and beggars sitting on the steps in rags,
counting their rosaries. It was his fate, however, to die a Jewish
martyr's death. In 1941, he was sent to the Warsaw Ghetto with
hundreds of other converts. Professor Pruszkowski rescued him
and hid him on the Aryan side of the city. Someone informed the
Gestapo who arrested another man by mistake. When Gotard
heard about this, he came out of hiding and gave himself up to free
the Pole mistakenly held. Gotard was sent to Treblinka, and
perished there.

Among Professor Pruszkowski's favorite students were two
talented painters with Biblical names: Menashe and Ephraim—
Zeidenbeitl— twins of the same height, the same hawk noses and
black hair, and always wearing the same clothes. It was impossible
to tell them apart. They were the chief attraction of the annual
artists' ball, held in the ruins of the royal castle in Kazimierz. When
one of them climbed into a covered box at one end of the ruins, to
emerge a second later from an identical box located at the other
end, the audience would burst into thunderous laughter. Only the
artists knew about the trick.

Among the older Jewish artists, who came back to Kazimierz
year after year and felt quite at home among the town's Jews, were

Henryk Berlevi, W. Weintraub, Abraham Ostrzega, Moshe Appelbaum, I. Tykocinksi, Vincent Brauner, Nathan Spiegel, I.
Rabinowicz, Feliks Friedman, Nathan Korzen, Chaim Hanft,
Joseph Shliwniak, and Jacob Rothbaum, who maintained a particularly close relationship with the town's youth. Kazimierz
produced two native artists, Samuel Wodnicki and the much
younger Chaim Goldberg. Wodnicki, a former yeshiva student
from a family which owned a store in the marketplace, attracted the
attention of visiting artists with his drawings of local subjects that
breathed spontaneity and a fresh charm, though they were
sometimes crudely executed. He settled in Palestine on the eve of
World War II and continued to draw scenes of his home town from
memory. Kazimierz was also the source of Chaim Goldberg's inspiration, although he did not confine himself to local themes. The son
of an extremely poor family in town, he dogged the footsteps of the
visiting artists during the summer months, helped carry their easels
and paint boxes, and silently observed how each one interpreted
the same fragment of landscape differently. They gave the enchanted youngster paint, brushes and paper, even bought his drawings and water colors, thus discreetly supporting him, and also
sponsored his studies at the art academies in Cracow and Warsaw.

At the outbreak of the war, Goldberg was called up by the Polish
army. He participated in the defense of Warsaw and managed to
reach the Soviet Union after Poland's collapse. During his stay in
the desolate wastes of Siberia, he was seized with an urge to
perpetuate the people and streets of his home town and made
drawings, oil paintings, wood carvings and metal sculptures, which
revealed his daring vision. After the Liberation Goldberg returned
to Poland and continued his work. He paid a last visit to Kazimierz,
saw that all trace of Jewish life had been erased, and settled in
Israel. There, like Samuel Wodnicki, he continued to paint scenes
of his home town from memory.

15

THE DESTRUCTION
OF KAZIMIERZ

In September 1939, Kazimierz suddenly surfaced on the war map of the crumbling Polish state. A procession of cars bearing members of the government, panic-stricken ministers of the Sanacja regime fleeing from Warsaw toward the Rumanian border, made an overnight stop there.

When the first Nazi bombs fell on Kazimierz soon afterward, a huge barge, floating down the Vistula from Cracow, dropped anchor near town with a cargo of twenty-seven crates. They contained the priceless treasure of the Royal Wawel Palace—golden crowns of Polish monarchs, medieval tapestries and paintings—and the symbol of Polish power, the sword of King Chrobry of the mighty Piast dynasty. In 1018, King Chrobry, an ancestor of Kazimierz the Great, had struck the gates of vanquished Kiev with this very saber during his victorious advance toward the east.

All the inhabitants of Kazimierz were involved in loading the huge crates of national relics onto wagons. In Pulawy and Deblin the Vistula had been blocked by bombed bridges so that the caravan wound its way through the side roads from Kazimierz to the

Rumanian border; from there it was sent to Canada where the treasures were preserved for the duration of the war.

It was a sunny autumn, the Kazimierz orchards were rich with ripe fruit, unusual abundance contrasting mockingly with the tragedy that was descending upon the town. At first it seemed as though the German occupation forces had forgotten about Kazimierz. Then the shtetl was suddenly roused by the news from neighboring Pulawy that the Nazis had issued a decree establishing a ghetto. It was late October 1939. This was perhaps one of the first orders concerning ghettoes to be issued in occupied Poland, at least in the Lublin Province, which had a primary role in the German plan to exterminate the Jewish population. The Nazi scheme was to turn Lublin into a region where the three-and-a-half million Polish Jews would be herded together. Pulawy was designated a "district seat" for thirteen neighboring towns, including Kazimierz. The Nazis quickly abandoned this plan. Yet the first death factories were built in the Lublin Province—Maidanek, Belzec and Sobibor.

In December 1939, the expulsion of the Pulawy Jews was implemented; they were driven into the ghettoes of neighboring towns, Wąwolnice, Konskowola, Riki and Opole. The order to set up a ghetto in Kazimierz was not issued until the spring of 1940; two of them were, in fact, established close to the marketplace, and Christians promptly took over Jewish stores and dwellings there. As in a number of other places, the composition of the German-appointed *Judenrat*—the Jewish Council— in Kazimierz dispels the widespread theory that all members were traitors or collaborators. The Kazimierz *Judenrat* consisted of the most respectable and responsible Jews of both the older and younger generations, the leaders of all the party organizations from the leftist Labor Zionists to the religious Mizrachi Party. Chaim Feuerstein was its chairman, the only member of that assimilated family to take part in community affairs. The secretary of the Council was Jonah Lustig, in whose house the only remaining Jewish inscription was uncovered after the war.

It was a year after the establishment of the ghetto in Kazimierz that my parents' last letter reached me. It was dated May 20, 1941. Its yellowed pages had become hardened from the black ink the Nazi censor had smeared over much of my father's spare, clear

Polish handwriting. This letter, which came to me in New York by way of San Francisco, begins with: "The only joy we have now is your happiness." Following this veiled hint, the censor's black mark extends over half-a-page to the words: "We no longer live in the house of the Brombergs . . ." Here the sentence is smudged again. The censor had apparently deleted my father's references to their new home in the ghetto. Nevertheless the return address on the envelope clearly indicated my parents' whereabouts: Ulica Nadrzeczna. This was the street that ran the length of the town's stream: the location of the second part of the ghetto, whose wooden shacks had previously been inhabited by Poles who had been assigned to the Jewish homes on the marketplace.

"Our only wish now," the letter continued, "is that we might see each other again. We pray to God for the war to end . . ." then another dark blot that extended down to the signatures of my father, mother, two brothers, their wives and children. The letter had not been mailed from Kazimierz, but from Pulawy, apparently with the help of a Polish friend who had undertaken this risky mission. The stamp bore the inscription "General Government" and the picture of the Royal Wawel Palace in Cracow, which was the residence of the Nazi governor-general, Dr. Hans Frank. There was also a postmark of a swastika gripped by an eagle's talons, and a signature: "Opened—*Oberkommando der Wehrmacht.*"

Of the eleven members of my family who signed this last message to me from the ghetto, only one managed to stay alive—a son of my eldest brother, Noah. In 1945, after the Nazi defeat, I received a note from him by way of an American officer. It began with: "Dearest Uncle! This is Pinia (Paul) writing to you. I am the only survivor of the whole family in Kazimierz . . ." The letter came from the newly-opened Displaced Persons camp in Landsberg, Germany, where my eighteen-year-old nephew now found himself on the last lap of a journey that had taken him through ghettos and slave camps where death had lurked constantly.

"Each time my strength failed me and I prayed for death," his letter continued, "I remembered my father's last note to me in Skarzysko. He wrote: 'My child, hold on. I believe that you will survive. Our whole family is gone. You will be the only one to tell how we perished.' "

At our first meeting in Landsberg, my nephew gave me a bundle of foolscap pages torn from a German bookkeeping ledger. The tiny Yiddish script covered the paper from edge to edge, leaving no margins. It was an endless sentence about the endlessness of Nazi crimes, of Jewish suffering, and of the world's indifference—an outburst of bitterness that spilled over the pages. It was a formless, scattered account of the various stages of hell my nephew endured after he escaped from the ghetto just before its liquidation. The time was March 1942; the efficiently run mass murders in Belzec where the Kazimierz Jews were being exterminated had reached their highpoint. Until then the town had been a forgotten island in a region from which Jews had long since been sent to the nearby death factories of Majdanek and Sobibor. Apart from the ghetto's overcrowded conditions, life in the *shtetl* rolled on more or less normally. The Jews even made fun of their own fate.

Paul Shneiderman described ghetto life by using a metaphor that originates from the landscape of Kazimierz. After the first spring rains, the mountainside crawls with countless snails of various sizes:

> "We were squeezed together like snails. But we continued our foolish lives in the tight rooms of Nadrzeczna Street. We even carried on our political discussions. One said Hitler had to lose, a second claimed that he would win, a third concluded: 'We lose anyway.' The pessimists weren't liked in the small ghetto, and were dubbed 'The Black Crows.' Sucher the Hunchback was particularly cheerful; he joked: 'Why blame Hitler? He's a kind man, as he's made all Jews equal. I, Sucher the Hunchback, and wealthy Chaim Feuerstein are equal now . . . It's better than it was before the war. After all, I live in the same palace as our aristocrats.' Discussions and jesting went on like this all day, until a Jewish policeman came to haul people off to forced labor. Then they scurried off into hiding."

This was the prevailing mood among the Kazimierz Jews just before the liquidation of the ghetto. Here is an account of the panic that seized people when the Nazis ordered the first deportation to the nearby town of Opole:

> "One fine morning a command to ship 500 Jews immediately came like a thunderbolt. The *Judenrat* was to organize the deportation with the help of the Jewish police. The crowd cried and pleaded; a few

scattered belongings were packed. Peasants swarmed in from everywhere to occupy Jewish homes. They would not let the owners take anything with them. You looked for Polish friends to hide you. They merely said: 'We'll watch over your belongings, but you must go with all the others.'

"My parents had permission to remain because I was working at the employment bureau, and my three brothers were laborers in the local stone quarry. My grandparents, Uncle Sholem, his wife and child had to go, however. I tried to intervene, but could do nothing for them. So I decided to go along. I might be able to help them somehow.

"In Opole we were met by mounted police. With yells and whiplashes, they forced the peasants to drive their human cargo faster to the hastily-built barracks. From afar I noticed two Nazis on horseback beating down on heads. I came up close and saw that one of them was Grandfather. I got several blows too, but managed to pull him off the wagon. I carried him into a barrack where men, women and children lay pressed close together on the floor. Grandfather rambled on so strangely that I realized his end was near. Grandmother was weeping; Sholem, his wife and child were crying too. All of a sudden, Grandfather opened his eyes and whispered to me: 'Piniele, save yourself. Remind the children to say *Kaddish* for me.' That's how he died.

"When I tried to leave the barrack, I found the door locked. There were no windows. I consulted with a few other young men who had also accompanied their elders, and we decided to dig our way out under the wall. After scratching away with our bare hands for several hours, we gouged out an opening and slipped out. We got back to Kazimierz and told them what had happened in Opole, and that people were sent on to Belzec from there. Those who remained in Kazimierz were sure, however, that nothing would happen to them. On March 30, a decree was issued for the final deportation."

The following day, the Passover eve exodus from Kazimierz began. It was the 13th day of Nissan, 5703, a Tuesday, the traditional market day, when long lines of wagons from the surrounding villages, laden with vegetables, fruit, dairy products, fowl, and calves would wind their way into town before dawn. On this Tuesday, March 31, 1942, the peasant carts arrived empty. They were to take the remaining Jews on their final journey—to Belzec. Some three hundred souls were herded into the marketplace. They had put the freshly baked *matzos* distributed by the community into their bundles. At the last moment a small group of Jews, the family of my eldest brother among them, managed to break through the police cordon encircling the marketplace. Led by Paul Shneiderman, they miraculously crossed the Vistula to Janowiec, where the ghetto was not to be liquidated until some months later. His account of this event was brief:

> "It is March 31. A gray dawn. A light spring rain accompanies us along the way. We come to the frozen Vistula, but it is impossible to cross it . . . The ice bursts with the echoes of cannonfire. The people moan and already want to turn back. Suddenly a powerful wind rises, a hurricane that pushes us forward and won't let us return. My father cries out: 'It's God's finger. With God's help we will cross!' For more than two hours we walk, literally jumping from floe to floe, which cracks beneath our feet until we reach the other shore."

Not a single witness has remained to describe the final exodus of Kazimierz Jewry, when the sick and elderly were loaded onto wagons, and the healthy walked to their own funerals in the gas chambers of Belzec.

Thirteen years later, when I visited Kazimierz, I was told about the heroic behavior of Israel Zilberminc, the town rabbi. Wearing his prayer shawl and carrying a Torah, he had chanted psalms as he walked beside the first wagon rolling out of the marketplace.

I left my home-town with the desolate feeling that the Jewish chapter in Kazimierz had come to an end, as it had in hundreds of other Polish *shtetlekh*, even though a few lonely Jews were staying on.

16

THE DEAD SHTETLEKH

I began my journey to the *shtetlekh* with the small communities radiating out from Warsaw: Grochow, Leszno, Ozarow, Truskow, Okuniew, and Marki-Pustelnik, whose Jewish population prided itself on its model gardeners. During the 1930's there were *hakhshara* stations (training centers) in Pustelnik for young *halutzim* ready to emigrate to the Land of Israel. Now I could not find a single Jew nor any trace of Jewish life. The catastrophe was only hinted at by the desolation of the marketplaces and the wild, overgrown gardens, where trees sagged under the weight of ripe apples, pears and plums. The boundaries between dream and reality often became blurred during my trip. I ceased being a simple observer who records facts and events that have no personal meaning for him. The ghastly experiences I heard about from surviving Jews often upset my equilibrium. The appalling stories about the *shtetlekh* invaded my dreams, giving me no rest.

The primitively modeled Christian shrines at the entrance to these *shtetlekh* had remained untouched in Communist Poland. In one place there was a bearded, naked Christ, a home-spun cotton towel draped across his thighs, a crown of thorns around his head. Elsewhere a madonna stood on a blue clay pedestal.

I gazed in the empty marketplaces, where Polish neighbors or peasants from nearby villages had "inherited" the stores of the vanished Jews. More than once I shivered as I found myself stepping on desecrated Jewish gravestones lying in a sidewalk puddle. My memory conjured up the image of the *shtetlekh* before the holocaust. The tiniest community of some hundred members had been a bastion of Jewish traditions and creative individuality regardless of their dire need and struggle for survival.

The small, wooden cottages on the Grochow marketplace were inhabited by gypsies. A metallic din reverberated through the town. It came from the shabby stone building that had once been a House of Prayer. It was the hammering from the gypsies' cooperative, where copper kettles, teapots, frying pans and bowls were being fashioned. On its eastern wall you could still detect the niche where the burned Holy Ark had nested. The once lively *shtetlekh* on the Otwock railroad line were also silent. I noticed only a few people in the streets and squares of Falenica, Josefow, Swider, and Otwock itself. Most of the private houses were decaying; only the larger villas that had served as guest houses had been converted into vacation homes for workers and state officials. I noticed, however, that some of the guest houses had barbed wire fences, and were patrolled by armed guards in civilian dress. I was told in confidence that these were the quarters for rather distinguished political prisoners who were kept under house arrest there.

Garwolin

I arrived in Garwolin at dawn. They were preparing for the weekly market. A dozen stands *(stragany,* as they were called) were set up, with yard goods, ready-made clothing, shoes, underwear and other consumer goods, tended by representatives of cooperatives, who had come from the larger towns round about. The only tradesmen to sell for private gain were those who offered foodstuffs: home-made sausage, baked goods, dairy products. Religious articles were on sale too—madonnas and pictures of saints, crosses, rosaries, and prayer books. Before the war, most of Garwolin's inhabitants had been Jews. Now I looked for one in vain.

The better brick houses sporting wrought iron balconies had not been destroyed; their trim was peeling, the stairs were decrepit, and the interiors looked gloomy. Wooden crosses and faded madonnas hung between beds. Here and there I could still see furniture obviously belonging to former Jewish tenants—solid oak credenzas and glass cupboards; the silver candlesticks and wine goblets, the *Hanukah* lamps and Passover dishes were gone.

Clothes and shoes were bought for the most part by the peasants who offered their products for sale at the Garwolin fair and then ate the traditional Polish borscht with meat in the smoke-filled local restaurant, where jugs of vodka stood ready on individual tables. I asked the owner whether any Jews lived in town. He said, yes, two, they had assumed Polish names: the lawyer Khinchevski, and Zembrovitch, secretary to the court. I met both of them in the courthouse and witnessed the wrangling of two peasants about the boundary between their adjoining properties—a dispute as old as Poland itself. Even now, in Communist Poland, such disputes are amongst the most common cases adjudicated in provincial courts, since agrarian reform in Poland permitted ownership of small parcels of land. Unfortunately, I found no opportunity to talk to the two lonely Jews. There was no recess; as in pre-war days, court was in continuous session on market days, so that peasants could have their grievances settled when they came to sell their produce or buy necessary goods.

We left this cheerless, half-ravaged town at dusk. Behind us the church bells' monotonous chimes mingled with the creaking of a wooden well-wheel, as a peasant by the roadside drew up a pail of water.

Jablonna

Upon our arrival in Jablonna bitter memories surfaced; a chapter in Jewish martyrology had been written here preceding the Nazi slave camps. My first impulse was to go to the site where over 10,000 Jewish enlisted men and officers had been interned during the 1920-21 war between Poland and Bolshevik Russia. Here and there one could still see the half-dismantled barracks of the huge military camp outside of the town.

This occurred shortly after Poland had regained her independence following 150 years of subjugation. The Polish Chief of Staff,
General Kazimierz Sosnkowski, falsely accused the Jews in his
army of mass treason. They were all pulled back from the front,
even the many physicians among them, shipped to Jablonna in
trucks, and placed behind barbed wire. More than 3,000 of them
died within a few months—of hunger and epidemics. In protest the
internees in the Jablonna camp composed a song fuming with
resentment against this crime, and Jewish youngsters sang it in
secret to the tune of the patriotic march of Pilsudski's legions: "We,
of the first brigade. . ."

For Polish Jews the name Jablonna has become synonymous
with independent Poland's first shameful deed. Ironically, the camp
had been set up in a town where Jews and gentiles had lived in
unusual harmony for generations.

A remaining token of those idyllic times is the rather original
wooden building in the middle of the marketplace. Count August
Potocki had had it put up as a trading center for the Jewish merchants, whom he had encouraged to settle in Jablonna, in the 1880's
after the second abortive Polish insurrection. Jan Bloch, banker
and economist of Jewish descent, was then manager of the estates
and enterprises of the Potocki family. Later he became one of the
distinguished tycoons in the country. He built the first railroads,
owned numerous industrial plants, and managed to continue writing on economics and sociology. His pacifist work in six volumes,
The Future War, gave him international renown. The marriage
between his daughter and the noted Polish writer, Baron Joseph
Wayssenhof, took place in Count Potocki's palatial home.

Although his parents had him baptized as a child, Jan Bloch
considered himself a Jew. He donated generously to Jewish charitable institutions, and carried on a correspondence with the founder
of political Zionism, Theodor Herzl, regarding the necessity of
doing scientific research on anti-Semitism. Bloch chastised Warsaw's wealthy Jews for their stinginess. He is credited with saying
that the Jews of Warsaw gave "as little as their enfeebled Jewish
hearts permitted."

Count Potocki's mansion now was in ruins. Only the traders'
center had been spared and converted into dingy apartments. I

caught sight of a faded inscription on one of the stores: "Abraham Magid, ironmonger."

Serock

The only object preserved from the old Jewish community of Serock is a hard-cover register bound in yellow parchment. For centuries Jewish births were recorded here. As I turned the pages, I felt I was holding the souls of the town's Jews. Not a single tombstone marked their memory. Irena Zakrzewska, an elderly, impoverished landowner, showed me the volume. The local historian, who had been commissioned by the town council to write a monograph for the 900th jubilee year of Serock, Mrs. Zakrzewska told me that a Jewish community and stone synagogue had existed as far back as the fourteenth century. The town stood at the confluence of the rivers Narew and Bug, which enabled Jewish traders to disseminate their goods to the villages of the Mazowsze Province. Though it was a poor, little town, Jewish Serock had well-established religious and secular institutions—a loan society, a Yiddish school, a library, a drama circle and choir, adult courses, and labor unions. Among the militant young Jews with the most varied political affiliations, the *halutz* movement was particularly strong; a significant number did indeed leave for Palestine in time.

The gifted poet-painter, Yossl Grossbart, hailed from Serock. While still young, he attracted attention among Jewish literary and artistic circles in Warsaw with his profoundly sorrowful poems about the *shtetl*. In the summer of 1939, he wrote a poem permeated with despair—his premonition of the holocaust:

> *The summer has fled with the last birds,*
> *The days have sucked in the grayness.*
> *The village has drawn together, huddled*
> *Like children clasping their mother.*
>
> *Dreary autumn has arrived,*
> *The sky is all patches–gray upon gray.*
>
> *There are more poor now than ever,*
> *Dread, lurking at every door.*
> *Reb Gdaliah's shutters are clamped shut,*
> *At times the dusk falls into dawn.*

There had been 4,000 Jews in Serock of a population of 6,000. Barely one hundred had survived. The majority, about sixty of them, emigrated to Israel. The others were scattered throughout the world. I moved about the sad, empty, narrow streets, accompanied by the shadows of Serock's vanished Jews. I went up and down the stairs of their wooden houses, listening to the vague reminiscences of my guide, Antoni Ribnicki, a pre-war public school teacher, who had been assigned to me by the president of the town council. He listed the names of the owners of homes on the marketplace as well as on Kosciuszko Street, the *shtetl's* main artery. Ribnicki had gray hair and was of medium height. He spoke with deference of the Serock rabbi, although he could not recall his name, depicting him as an imposing figure with a snow-white beard. My guide also showed me a house with a wrought-iron balcony, where a wonder-rebbe had lived in the twenties and had created quite a stir in Serock. Ribnicki used the expression "holy miracle worker" and talked about him as if he were a figure in the very distant past. The former teacher also brought to life various episodes of the recent past in Serock, of which no trace could be seen anywhere.

Serock had gained renown in the Jewish world during the second half of the 19th Century, when the brilliant Rabbi Joseph Levenstein settled there. He occupied the rabbinical chair for half-a-century, from 1874 to 1924, and managed to live a creative life in this tranquil little town, which could not be reached even by train. He wrote many religious commentaries that have taken a significant place in modern rabbinical literature, and apart from his commentaries on the Torah and the Talmud, he created a towering work, a kind of rabbinical encyclopedia comprising 6,600 biographies of rabbis and hasidic *rebbes*.

The "holy man" mentioned by my guide was the young *Rebbe* Aaron Katzenelnbogen. In 1926, during the week of Passover, he had abruptly called upon his disciples to go and meet the Messiah near the "Napoleonic Hills" outside Serock. Katzenelnbogen claimed that he was a descendant of the Baal Shem Tov, founder of the hasidic movement. He had come to Serock from a small town in Volynia at the close of World War I. The poor immediately gathered around the young *rebbe*—butchers, coachmen, peddlers and porters. His disciples whispered that he studied Kabbalah day and night, yet he did not give the impression of a mystic. His blond beard neatly groomed, he was always decked out in a long, silk frock coat, kid boots, and an expensive fur-edged hat. His wife was considered a beauty, and was elegantly dressed.

The old Rabbi of Serock, Joseph Levenstein, had serious doubts about the young *rebbe's* conduct, but kept silent out of tolerance. After his death, however, the hasidic *Rebbe* Abraham Yitzhak Morgenstern, of the Kotzk dynasty, took over Rabbi Levenstein's court. Then the feud began. Acting in accordance with the traditions of Kotzk, where they did not believe in performing miracles, the new *rebbe* began to contest the practices of the Serock miracle worker. The struggle flared up in particular when Rebbe Katzenelnbogen suddenly had himself called "The Serocker Preacher." At the Third Sabbath Meal* he began to assert that messianic times were drawing near and that people should prepare themselves for the great day of redemption. He sent for the town tailor, the well-to-do Yossl Grzebieniarz, who made clothes for the wealthy residents of the region, including Prince Radziwill, and ordered several silk frock coats in the brightest colors—blue, green and red. He also had a tall, red hat made, onto which a mystical symbol was sewn. All of this occurred in the winter of 1926.

On the seventh day of Passover, the Serocker Preacher used to conduct the Additional Morning Prayers in the main synagogue. After the reading of the Torah, he unexpectedly told the congregation that he would heal the sick that day. After services they all went out into the street. Dancing and singing, they marched toward the marketplace. The *rebbe* came out on his balcony, dressed in all his opulence, and spoke to the crowd below, hinting that the Messiah would appear within the next few days. His Hasidim gathered the town's sick together. There was a young man among them, son-in-law of a baker, who had suffered from the sleeping sickness. A survivor of Jewish Serock, Shmuel Bruckanski, witnessed as a boy the following bizarre scene: when the *rebbe* cried out, "Get up and

---

*At dusk, the *rebbe* and his Hasidim hold a prolonged session over a scant repast, interpreting the Torah and intoning *nigunim,* sacred melodies.

walk!", to everyone's amazement, the sick man rose and walked. News of the miracle spread fast to the surrounding towns. Jews came from all over to seek the *rebbe's* help. Tales of his miracles ceased, however, when he ordered a sick baby to be circumcised, and the child died. Then he sank into a deep depression, became ill himself, and died soon after.

My guide took me to the Warsaw road, in order to show me the Jewish cemetery and the monument on the grave of the Serock Rabbi, Joseph Levenstein. But there was no trace of it. Where the cemetery had been, freshly-ploughed fields stretched away from us, and in the stillness of the early autumn Sunday afternoon, we could hear the splashing of the River Narew.

Pultusk

Pultusk was a chartered town as far back as 1257. Jews figured among its early settlers and, in the 15th century, it was a Jew who established one of Poland's first printing shops there. A volume of sermons by the venerable priest, moralist and witty polemicist, Piotr Skarga, came off the hand press. As head of the Jesuit Order, he lived in Pultusk during the second half of the 16th century, and was then called to Cracow to serve as preacher at the court of Sigismund III. For hundreds of years, Skarga's name was bound up with the daily life of Pultusk's Jewish community. The ancient stone synagogue and the ritual bath were located on Piotr Skarga Street; hasidic houses of prayer, religious schools, and a cooperative bank had been added later. Artisans and shopkeepers lived there, too; for Skarga Street was the home of the town's poorer Jews. Not a single sign of that life remains. The wooden houses have gone up in smoke, nothing but a pile of stones indicated the site of the old synagogue, yet the inscription, "Street named after Piotr Skarga," can still be read on a wall at the corner.

Despite its 500-year history, the rather well-to-do community of Pultusk produced neither religious nor secular personalities as had other smaller *shtetlekh* of the region. Only Reb Leizerl of Pultusk gained fame; during the violent period of the 1863 uprising, he urged his congregation to support the Polish struggle for freedom from czarist rule.

The town is one of the most exceptional middle-sized towns of Poland. The marketplace with its historic structures is situated on an island on the River Narew, like the Ile de la Cité on the River Seine in Paris. Jews had lived there in relative peace for centuries, but when Poland became independent, it was shaken by the boycott movement and by anti-Semitic harassments. An unusual item published in 1928 in the local Yiddish weekly *Undzer Vort* testified to the degree of discrimination against Jews by the administration of the town: "A Jewish woman clerk has started working in the municipal offices." It must have been an important event in that county capital where, out of 20,000 inhabitants, more than 7,000 were Jewish. Pultusk was a cultural center for the surrounding Jewish towns and villages. *Undzer Vort,* one of the country's best Yiddish weeklies, was edited by the gifted poet Simhah Dan, who later died in a concentration camp. The town had a private Jewish high school and a large choral society with its own orchestra, and apart from the big, independent I. L. Peretz Library, each political group—Zionist Revisionists, the People's Party, Left and Right Poale Zionists, and the social democratic *Bund*—had its own library. The drama circle produced the most important works of Jewish playwrights, and put on guest performances in nearby *shtetlekh*. Jews were spared in larger numbers than in any other community in Poland. About 5,000 of the 7,000 survived all over the world, approximately 3,000 in Israel; not a single Jew has chosen to stay in his home town.

The miracle that saved so many of Pultusk's Jews came about through tremendous suffering and sacrifice. Nine days after Germany attacked Poland, the town was occupied by the *Reichswehr,* who straightaway warned the Jewish inhabitants: "We shall not harm you. But we're not staying here long. The SS and Gestapo will follow, and they will destroy you." The pogrom began on the first day of Rosh Hashanah, the New Year Holy Day, when a band of SS men raided Yohanan's Hasidic Court, and chased the men out into the street. Gentile barbers were ordered to cut off half their beards on one side and half their hair on the other. Then they drove the Jews down Senatorska Street, and filmed the wretched procession. The expulsion from the town was ordered on the eve of *Sukkot,* the Feast of Tabernacles. The entire Jewish population was to leave within several hours, taking none of their possessions with them. Since most of them were in the synagogue at the time, they were chased out to the Wyszkow Route. The moment they were squeezed onto the bridge over the River Narew the Nazis machine-gunned them from the castle tower, and dropped incendiary bombs on them. Hundreds of Jews were turned into living torches, and died in agony. The rest fled in the direction of the new Russian border, which the Soviet-German partition of Poland had fixed in the town of Zarąb. When they arrived there, Soviet soldiers gave them a friendly reception, and distributed bread among them. As an additional welcome, a military band was playing in the marketplace. From there the refugees were conducted to Bialystok, and later evacuated to various parts of the Soviet Union.

After the war ended, in 1945-46, most of the survivors joined the first large-scale repatriation to Poland. When the Kielce pogrom took place on July 4, 1946, they were among the first to flee to the Displaced Persons Camps in Germany. From there they emigrated to Israel and to other countries.

The striking remnants of this ancient Jewish community are the stone, fortress-like houses on the marketplace, built in late Renaissance style. They had been put up by Jewish merchants who exported grain to Danzig in exchange for porcelain, amber and other luxury items for the landowners of the province.

Amshinov

If a foreign Jew were to come to this town and read the sign marked "Mszczonow," he would hardly guess that this is the old *shtetl*, Amshinov, where the son of Reb Yitzhak Vorker had founded the hasidic dynasty of the Amshinov *rebbes*.

I first visited Amshinov in 1927, some days after the death of the renowned Yiddish poet, novelist and playwright, H. D. Nomberg, who had been born there. The main street hummed like a beehive; door after door on both sides belonged to scores of small Jewish shops and larger businesses. Men with all kinds of beards and earlocks moved swiftly among the peasant customers from outlying villages. They wore long, black gabardines and round hats, which often barely concealed skullcaps set low on the napes of their necks. Groups of young people stood around in the market-

Wooden synagogue in Lanckorona (destroyed).

place. Some had carefully trimmed beards, others were clean-shaven; some still wore the traditional round hats, some had cycling caps on, others wore modern hats. They argued about which of the town's types Nomberg had immortalized, calling his characters by their true names. Someone told the following story: Years before, on a visit to his home town, Nomberg had been attacked by one of his protagonists, who had recognized himself as the hero in a story. He was a giant, and threw himself upon the weak, little man, his fists outstretched. Luckily, Nomberg was accompanied by friends who protected him.

His maternal grandfather, Aaron Eisenberg, had been a success-ful timber merchant who spent several months a year in Danzig. He traded with the landowner of a large estate nearby called Bobsk, and used to drive around town in a coach drawn by four horses. He was also chief of the town's fire brigade, and rode a horse in traditional Jewish attire, astonishing the local population. It was from this grandfather that Nomberg had inherited his lust for life and intense curiosity about the world.

Posters in the Amshinov marketplace announcing his death had been hung up by the local branch of the People's Party, of which Nomberg had been co-founder. I saw them on all the roads and side streets of the town except the one where the synagogue was, the bailiwick of Rabbi Joseph Kalish. Some hot-tempered Hasidim had come to blows with members of the People's Party who had attemp-ted to affix the obituary to the wall of Nomberg's birthplace which adjoined the *rebbe's* court.

As a *yeshiva* student, Nomberg took his Hebrew verses to I. L. Peretz in Warsaw, who was the idol of the new generation of Yiddish writers, and the great poet prevailed upon him to write in Yiddish as well. The conflicts within Nomberg's soul between his orthodox roots and progressive ideas found expression in his lucid rationalism and profound lyrical pessimism. The characters in his tales represented their author's skepticism and soul-searchings.

On my 1957 visit to Amshinov after an absence of more than thirty years, I found the street, the synagogue and Nomberg's family home unchanged. The *shtetl* had been spared. The town's Jews had been herded into the ghetto of neighboring Rawa-Mazowiecka, and had died there. I also found the impressive house

owned by his grandfather—a wooden dwelling with a large, chiscl-
led porch. The buildings in the *rebbe's* court had escaped devasta-
tion as well. A cobblers' cooperative had been set up in the stone
synagogue. The tall-windowed dwellings of the *rebbe's* large family were now occupied by Polish workers, mostly from other
places, who had settled there during the Nazi occupation. At the
corner of that street was a pitiful privately owned grocery store—
one of the few in Amshinov that was opened after the October 1956
revolt, when the Gomulka regime liberalized the ban on "private
enterprise." I bought a pound of apples. The owner, a man in his
sixties, told me that he had known the *shtetl's* last *rebbe*, Joseph
Kalish, who died shortly before the outbreak of the war.

"I supplied the *rebbe* with wood," he said. "I'd stack cords of
lumber in his court as early as summertime. I knew the *tzadik* well.
[He actually used this Hebrew word for saintly man.] He was a
wise man. Even the landlord of the etate nearby, Bobsk, thought
highly of him and sowed an acre of wheat especially for him, so that
he'd have flour for Passover *matzo*.

"We Poles," confessed the grocer, "sure committed sins against
our Jews. [He used the Polish diminutive, *zydki*.]. And our present
lot is God's punishment upon us. All we ever did was to blame the
Jews for everything. We're only now realizing that while the Jews
lived among us we Poles lived much better. We made our livelihood
from them. When the name of our town was Amshinov, the Jewish
name for it, things were hopping here. But now, you can see for
yourself what our Mszczonow looks like—it's a town that's half
dead."

Rawa-Mazowiecka

The *shtetlekh* that no longer harbored a single Jew seemed less
tragic than those where a handful had stayed on. I felt this when I
came to the historic town, Rawa-Mazowiecka, after leaving *iuden-
rein* Amshinov. There were only three survivors here out of a
Jewish population of over 6,000 that had lived in this once-bustling
trading center: the widow Leah Hoffnung, her 10-year-old daughter, Rose, and Moshe Broner. He had married the gentile woman
who had hidden him after the ghetto was liquidated in 1942 and a
year later had joined the partisans in the forests. As a reward, the

town council allocated to Broner a piece of land that had formerly belonged to the Jewish community. It was the site of the old wooden synagogue which was burned down as soon as the Nazis had entered the town. In return for the privilege of working this parcel of land, on which he and his wife were cultivating vegetables, Broner had accepted the responsibility of looking after the Jewish cemetery. He took me there, and proudly pointed out the fence and tombstones he had himself repaired. He had transferred several 17th and 18th century monuments from the demolished old cemetery. Bitterly he pointed out the freshly-turned earth of graves where "human hyenas" had searched for gold teeth.

Broner invited me to his home. He lived on the marketplace in a stone house with neo-Gothic vaults. It was Friday evening. As we mounted the steps, I was met by the sweet and peppery smell of freshly-cooked Sabbath fish. Mrs. Broner opened the door and to my amazement spoke to us in fluent Yiddish. There were two tall, silver candlesticks on the table, ready to be lit. On the heavy oaken sideboard stood a brass *Hanukah* candelabrum. I noticed about a score of Yiddish books in a glass-enclosed bookcase. They included the works of Sholem Aleichem, I. L. Peretz, Abraham Reisin, and younger Yiddish writers. The cabinet also contained a Bible, a Passover *Haggadah*, and prayer books. On the wall above the Israeli calendar hung a photograph of a distinguished old man wearing a skullcap. His ample, bifurcated snow-white beard mingled with his thick earlocks. Before I was able to ask who he was, Mrs. Broner enlightened me. It was the Rabbi of the town, Yerahmiel Moshe Noah Rappaport, who had been killed by the Nazis.

Mrs. Broner then ran off to fetch the lonely Jewish widow, Leah Hoffnung, who came after a while with her daughter, Rose. Mrs. Hoffnung had no complaints about making a living, but their loneliness was unbearable, and she was filled with anxiety for Rose, the only Jewish child in her school.

"Tell the guest how they plague you!" The mother held out her arms to her daughter. The girl shyly turned her head away and said nothing; but her mother urged her on, and she told us how her schoolmates called "Zydowa" (Jewess) after her when she left the room at the beginning of the religion class. (Voluntary religious instruction was introduced into Polish public schools after the October 1956 revolt, and religion classes had resulted in the baiting of those Jewish pupils who did not attend.) Rose added that her schoolmates had rarely played with her before religious studies were reintroduced. Since then school had become sheer hell.

The Nazis had set up three separate ghettos in different sections of Rawa-Mazowiecka. Apart from the town's Jews, others from neighboring *shtetlekh* had been herded together there—from Amshinov, Mogelnitz, and Biala-Rawska. On October 28, 1942, all three ghettoes were liquidated, and their inmates departed to Treblinka and Auschwitz. Leah Hoffnung was sent to Treblinka, her husband, Michael, to Auschwitz. After their liberation they returned to Rawa-Mazowiecka, and had their daughter. She was hardly three years old when her father died in 1950. Leah Hoffnung, her daughter Rose, and Moshe Broner were the last remaining Jews of a community that had grown in Rawa-Mazowiecka since the Middle Ages.

There was no visible trace of the centuries-old Jewish communal buildings. Yet the town boasts some remarkable medieval structures, of which the foremost is the armory with its tall, red brick tower; it belonged to the Prince of Mazowsze, who governed the Mazowsze province at the beginning of the 14th Century. Events took place in Rawa-Mazowiecka that have reverberated throughout all of Europe. Invited by the Prince to hunt in the dense forests round about, mighty rulers gathered there.

Local romances found their way into world literature. Shakespeare's *The Winter's Tale* is based on the family tragedy of Prince Ziemowit III who, out of jealousy, locked his pregnant wife into the armory tower. Soon after the countess gave birth to a daughter in captivity, she committed suicide. Though Shakespeare set his play at the court of the King of Sicily, literary historians have established that he adopted the plot from an old English novel based upon the Rawa-Mazowiecka incident. This story also served as a plot for a number of Polish novels.

Jewish merchants were well established in Rawa-Mazowiecka even before the reign of Prince Ziemowit III. The town's earliest archives are replete with names of Jews who built a large community there in the 16th Century. But during the frequent skirmishes among the princely rulers of the surrounding provinces, the Jews were always the first victims. At various times, Rawa-Mazowiecka was burned down by invading German and Swedish armies. The Jews were expelled repeatedly, and their communal centers razed, but they always returned, rebuilt their homes, and transferred monuments from wrecked cemeteries to the new one. That was what Moshe Broner had done once again—perhaps for the last time.

Tomaszow-Mazowiecki

The destruction of the Jewish community of Tomaszow-Mazowiecki is embodied in its rebuilt main street—a splendid, broad avenue bordered by restored houses and tastefully decorated shops. It is called Liberation Avenue. Its name and the monument erected there commemorate the Red Army's casualties during the battle to liberate the town from the Nazis. Its name before the war was "Avenue of the Polish Army"; it had been the center of Jewish commercial activity in this modern textile town. I looked for a Jewish store in vain, but I did come across sorrowful traces: ravaged gravestones had been used to build the Soviet obelisk, whose Russian inscription proclaimed: "Eternal Glory for the Freedom Fighters." Gentile residents who had witnessed the erection of the obelisk told me the story of the Jewish cemetery's profanation. Before the Red Army arrived, tombstone engravers robbed the cemetery, and then supplied the marble and granite slabs for the Soviet monument.

The outbreak of World War II and subsequent Nazi occupation affected Tomaszow differently from most other Polish towns. It was bombed by German planes well before the population learned that the Nazis had attacked Danzig on Friday, September 1, 1939, and just five days later—on Wednesday, September 6—the German army captured Tomaszow. Over 1,000 Polish subjects of German origin, the "Volksdeutsche," who had maintained peaceful relations with their Jewish neighbors, dropped their masks at the Nazis' entry into Tomaszow. As privileged German nationals, they immediately took to plaguing and persecuting defenseless Jews. As early as December 22, 1939, the Jewish population of Tomaszow was forced to wear the Jewish emblem—a white armband with a blue Star of David on it. Yet the ghetto was established later than in any other town of occupied Poland; not until January 1942 did the Nazis order barbed wire put up around the four streets inhabited by Jews: 15,000 local Jewish residents plus several thousand others from adjacent towns were herded into that cramped area. Well before the ghetto was set up, the Nazis succeeded in torturing hundreds of Tomaszow Jews; they died while building roads and clearing forests. The ghetto lasted for two years. By the end of 1943, its population was deported to the Treblinka extermination camp.

The highly gifted, 20-year-old poet-painter, Tadeusz Bornstein, wrote and painted feverishly in those last months before his death in the ghetto. He had rejected his Polish friends' offers to hide him on the "aryan" side of town, because he would not part from his mother.

Only a few hundred Tomaszow Jews came out of the concentration camps alive; most emigrated to Israel directly from Germany, and about thirty returned to their home town after the Liberation of Poland and attempted to revive their communal life. The Kielce pogrom of 1946 destroyed their last hopes, and most of them left the country too. In the winter of 1957, one more lonely Jew joined the five remaining ones: Dr. Fabian Warszawski, a man in his seventies, just set free from a Soviet labor camp in Siberia and repatriated to Poland.

One of the youngest towns in Poland. Tomaszow-Mazowiecki was founded during the mid-19th Century when Europe experienced the sweep of the Industrial Revolution, the period known as the "Spring of Nations." It was built by Count Tomasz Ostrowski, who lived in France and Britain for a time. His dream was that the town be named for him and become a combination of Paris and Manchester. He made sure that Tomaszow would not develop in the same chaotic manner as nearby Lodz, with its narrow streets and jerry-built architecture. A worldly man with progressive ideas, he wanted his town to be open to all nationals and invited Jewish artisans and businessmen as well as German, Russian and Swedish colonists. Tomaszow became a truly integrated community of people with different backgrounds who felt they were partners in their town's prosperity. At the close of the 19th Century, the wealthier Jews of the town gave their support to the blossoming of modern Hebrew literature. This was largely due to the influence of Nahum Sokolov, the Hebrew writer and scholar from Wyszogrod who, at 20 years of age, was famous in all of Poland. Many of the Jewish merchants had Sokolov tutor their children, and during his brief stay in Tomaszow, from 1879 to 1880, he won local support for the development of Hebrew culture, particularly for the daily *Ha-tzefirah* (The Dawn), whose editor he became at the age of 21.

The second generation of Tomaszow Jews became thoroughly assimilated and donated funds to Polish art and literature. In the period between the two world wars, the textile merchants' mansions were "home" to avant-garde Polish writers and artists, among whom there were many Jews, and chief among these was the great poet, Julian Tuwim. He had been born in Lodz, but spent his most creative years in nearby Tomaszow. It was there that he revealed his mastery of the Polish language. He also taught the children of the Jewish textile manufacturers in the town, where he met his future wife, Stephanie Marchev, who was known as a rare beauty. The countryside around—the river banks of the Pilica, the pine forests, lakes and far-flung fields—all these give one a sense of how Julian Tuwim, stemming from the smoke-ridden and prosaic Lodz, was able to introduce such astoundingly fresh images and pure lyricism into the new Polish poetry of the twenties.

Tomaszow, a stronghold of orthodox Judaism, had religious schools of all levels. When Poland became independent, all the secular parties set up their own distinctive schools and clubs, and an excellent weekly began to appear. The fine actress, Clara Segalovitch, came to the modern Yiddish theater from Tomaszow. The beautiful, temperamental Clara was born in Kharbin, the Far East, and, as a young girl, had moved to the town with her parents.

When I visited Tomaszow in 1958 and asked whether there were any Jews in the town, I was referred to Shmuel Tolman, an official at the local planning agency. He immediately took time off, led me to the ruined streets of the former ghetto, and invited me to his house, which he had turned into a museum for Jewish martyrology. The walls were covered with photographs depicting ghetto life, especially deportation scenes. He had found pictures of the bones

of underground fighters shot in surrounding fore
and buried in the Jewish cemetery after the Libe
covered with a wrinkled curtain from the ar
synagogue. A broken brass *menorah* and a
stood there—the last things to be dug up
ghetto.

Piotrkow

Millions of Bibles, sets of the Talmud, prayer books, and a
deal of Yiddish literature had been published in Piotrkow
handful of Jews who survived and returned could not find a
siddur or any other Jewish book there. During the German
bardment of Piotrkow in September 1939, fires that broke out i
Jewish quarter continued to burn for weeks, fed by the book
which the town was renowned throughout the Jewish world.
volumes that were saved were later destroyed by the Nazis,
seized the lead type and made the typesetters remove the ink so
the letters could be converted into clean bullets.

I looked in vain for a Jewish face in the streets of this
community, where over 15,000 Jews had lived at the beginning
World War II. On Garncarska, Jerozolimska and Staro-W
szawska, once all Jewish streets, my question to passersby abc
where Jews lived was met with astonishment. There was just o
Jewish name in the town's telephone directory: Dr. Sigmu
Tenenbaum. I called it repeatedly. There was no answer.

As I walked through Tribunal Square which had at one tin
served as the heart of Jewish Piotrkow, a well-dressed, elegant
groomed, elderly Pole with a long beard came towards me. Whe
he noticed my interest in the small, recently-restored Renaissanc
houses, he remarked with pride: "Warsaw can't put our old town t
shame, can it?"

I asked the friendly old man whether he knew where the Jewish
inhabitants in town lived. He tugged nervously at his square beard
and, as if caught off guard, said:

"No Jews live here now."

In the 14th Century, Piotrkow was the seat where the Polish
Parliament (the Sejm), the synods, and the royal tribunal convened.